Coral Seas

Coral Seas

Roger Steene

FIREFLY BOOKS

For Shirley, Christine and Christine, together at last.

A FIREFLY BOOK

Copyright © 1998 Roger Steene

Firefly Books acknowledges the financial support of the Government of Canada through the Book Publishing Industry Development Program for our publishing activities.

Cataloguing in Publication Data

Steene, Roger C.
   Coral Seas

ISBN 1-55209-290-9

1. Coral reef biology – Australia – Great Barrier Reef (Qld.) – Pictorial works.
2. Great Barrier Reef (Qld.) – Pictorial works. I. Title.

QH197.S73   1998   578.77'89476   C98-930838-3

Published in Canada in 1998
by Firefly Books Ltd.
3680 Victoria Park Avenue
Willowdale, Ontario, Canada
M2H 3K1

Published in the United States in 1998
by Firefly Books (U.S.) Inc.
P.O. Box 1338, Ellicott Station
Buffalo, New York, USA
14205

Produced and published in Australia in 1998
by Crawford House Publishing Pty Ltd
P.O. Box 1484
Bathurst NSW 2795, Australia

Printed and bound by Toppan Printing Company Ltd, in Singapore

Captions for preceding pages

Pages ii-iii: Fringing reefs surround low volcanic islands in Palau. Over eons
they will gradually sink, but the corals will grow upwards resulting in a series of atolls.
Aerial, Palau.

Pages iv-v: Red Sea reefs offer a startling contrast with the adjacent land. Barren desert terrain plunges suddenly into
a watery universe, literally exploding with marine life.
Ras-umm-Said, Sharm-el-Sheikh, Red Sea, Egypt.

Pages vi-vii: Coral islets present a microcosm of life. Once vegetation takes hold
on an emergent platform of beachrock and sand, it quickly attracts colonising organisms. This process duplicates the
ecological succession taking place below the waves.
Massas Island, Madang, Papua New Guinea.

Pages viii-ix: The passing years magically convert an ugly cargo container into
a spectacular coral garden. In time this structure will collapse under the
weight of the encroaching growths and its presence will be hidden forever.
Jolanda Reef, Sharm-el-Sheikh, Red Sea, Egypt.

Acknowledgements

I am indebted to my constant diving companion, Dr Jerry Allen, for his interest and enthusiasm in my projects during countless field trips over the years. Jerry is the author of twenty-five books, and his suggestions and advice have often lifted my casual observations to a more meaningful and scientifically interesting level. Jerry's exploits and achievements have become legendary in the Southwest Pacific in the marine and freshwater spheres. I wish to also thank him for his valuable assistance in the preparation of this book.

To Dr Walter Starck, many thanks for wonderful memories, dives and field trips on your unique research vessel *El Torito* before its recent retirement. Also grateful thanks for the input into this volume.

Special thanks are due to Peter Parks of Image Quest 3 – D, United Kingdom, who introduced me to the wonderful world to be seen through a microscope. Among many attributes, Peter is an authority on the use of high-magnification systems to record the unseen marvels of nature. Most of the equipment he uses he has invented and developed himself. He kindly allowed me to use his unique optical bench with its photographic system and demonstrated innovative techniques to assist me in obtaining images of plankton, large and small, during late-night sessions at the Lizard Island Research Station on the Great Barrier Reef, Australia.

Dr Pat Colin allowed me to use his aerial photo of an atoll, something I was unable to achieve despite numerous attempts foiled by bad weather. Denise Nielsen-Tackett contributed the tenth image in the 'Wonderpuss' series. Nobuo Suda photographed the white whale.

Rudie H. Kuiter shared multiple dives and photo subjects and constantly assisted with his awesome knowledge of electronics.

I would also like to thank: Lynn and Lance Adrian; Dr Phil Alderslade; Drs Avril and Tony Ayling; Brian Bailey; Dr and Mrs H. Batuna, Murex Dive; Resort, Manado, Indonesia; Fred Bavendam; Dr David Bellwood; Max Benjamin, Walindi Dive Resort, Papua New Guinea; Dr Sandy Bruce; Rick and Do Cammick, Dive Taveuni, Fiji; Denise Carlson; Dr Marc Chamberlain; Dr Pat Colin and Lori Bell-Colin, Coral Reef Research Foundation, Palau; Ian Croll; Dr Peter Davie; His Excellency The Dorcas of Ibis; Mark Ecenbarger, Kungkungan Bay Resort, Sulawesi, Indonesia; Dr Daphne Fautin; Dr Terry Gosliner; Scott Harmon; Dr Vicki Harriott; Dr Douglas Hoese; Ron Holland, Borneo Divers, Sabah, Malaysia; Dr John Hooper; Dr Pat Hutchings; Dr Matthew Jebb; Burt Jones and Maurine Shimlock; Nyoman and Reno Kirtya, Grand Komodo Tours, Bali, Indonesia; Toshikazu and Junko Kozawa, Anthis Corp., Japan; Jimmy Krakode (AIDC); Mike Lark; Dr Jim Lowry; Loisette Marsh; Dr Patricia Mather; Scott and Janine Michael; Dr Kal Muller; Phil and Kathy Munday; Dr Mark Norman; James Dennis O'Doherty; Dr Larry Orsak, Christensen Research Institute, Madang, Papua New Guinea; Carol Palmer and Sonny Tjandra, Ambon Dive Centre, Indonesia; Dr Hannelore Paxton; Austin. K. Peacrab; Tad Perkage; Alan Raabe, Fe Brina Dive Cruises, Walindi, Papua New Guinea; Dr John E. Randall; Dr Ross Robertson; Dr Frank Rowe; Anton Saksono; Sao Wisata Resort, Maumere, Flores, Indonesia; Joseph Schaffelner; Larry Sharron; Cody Shwaiko; Wally Siagian; Throti Singha; Shirley Slack-Smith; Larry Smith; Lyle Squire Sr, Lyle Squire Jr, and Cadel Squire; Nobuo Suda; Larry Tackett and Denise Nielsen-Tackett; Kornholio Van Thou; Nick Tonks, Reef Image Plaza, Cairns, Australia; Takamasa Tonozuka, Dive and Dive's, Bali, Indonesia; Dr Tom and Anmarie Tomascik; Mark Turdett; Dr Lyle Vail and Anne Hoggett, Lizard Island Research Station, Australia; Dr Charlie Veron; Wakatobe Divers, Tolandono, Tukang Besi, Indonesia; Dr Gary Williams.

Introduction

Coral reefs are without doubt one of our planet's greatest natural attractions. Having spent my entire life virtually on the threshold of the Great Barrier Reef, I have a certain temptation to take the reef and all its wonders for granted. After all, I've spent countless hours diving there. But instead, I'm humbled on every visit. Just think about the phenomenal forces of nature that could shape such an incredible structure. The Great Barrier Reef and every other coral reef in the world are the end result of a magical interplay of chance factors.

Clear warm seas and sun-drenched shallows are two of the prime ingredients for coral reef development. These conditions promote abundant plant growth, which provides the basic fuel for corals and a host of other organisms. Most of the plant component is not obvious to a first-time reef visitor. The majority is in the form of a fine filamentous coating that covers bare rocky surfaces or is even less conspicuous, living within the tissues of a variety of invertebrates such as sponges, corals, molluscs, and sea squirts. These microscopic, single-celled algae are known as 'zooxanthellae'. Like all plants they depend on sunlight for photosynthesis, a process which uses the sun's energy to make sugar from carbon and water. The sugar is then 'leaked' to the coral, or other invertebrate host, providing it with energy for growth. This is why the majority of corals thrive in shallow water where sunlight is optimal.

The magnificent living corals that are so obvious when we visit places like the Great Barrier Reef are just a small part of the overall reef structure. They form a relatively thin veneer that encrusts a solid platform of limestone, composed of skeletal remains of past coral generations and numerous reef-dwelling organisms that had hard parts or shells composed of calcium carbonate. Major non-coral contributors to this matrix include molluscs, crustaceans, echinoderms, foraminifera, sponges, worms, and fishes, as well as certain plants that secrete calcium carbonate (most notably green algae of the genus *Halimeda*).

Coral reefs are sometimes compared to tropical rainforests due to their great ecological complexity and abundance of species (biodiversity). But even the much-heralded rainforest pales in comparison, at least in terms of readily observed animal life. No other ecological system on earth can boast such a large and diverse cast of

Opposite: Reef from the air, Palau.

Hermit crab with its protective shell.
Aniculus sp. (6 cm), in 10 m,
Lembeh Straits, Sulawesi, Indonesia.

Colony of raspberry tunicates.

Didemnid (5 mm), in 12 m,

Tulamben, Bali, Indonesia.

characters. The coral reef literally oozes life. In addition to the obvious community of plants and animals seen on or above the surface of the reef, there are literally thousands of unseen organisms. Hundreds of species may be associated with a single small coral-head, not to mention the legions found under rocks, among dead coral slabs, or in the myriad crevices and fissures. There are also unseen communities of microscopic organisms living on the reef's surface, under sand, and in the water column directly above.

The antiquity of coral reefs is equally impressive as the physical forces that shape them. Fossil evidence shows us that reefs are an extremely ancient phenomena. They first appeared more than 400 million years ago. Although these original corals became extinct eons ago, they set the stage for the evolution of modern forms. Actually, it was not until the past 25 million years (a recent event on the geological time scale) that modern forms made their appearance. Today's coral reefs – exemplified by the Great Barrier Reef – were primarily built during the past 5000 years or even faster, a mere drop in the bucket as far as earth's time scale is concerned.

There is growing concern about the rapid decline of coral reefs, particularly in Southeast Asia. Fishing with explosives has caused widespread destruction. The severity of this problem was highlighted during a recent visit to northern Borneo (Sabah). I heard (and felt!) underwater explosions on almost every dive. I also witnessed scores of 'bald spots' where coral was destroyed by previous blasting. Clearly, it's up to local governments to eliminate these destructive practices, but of course this is easier said than done.

At the other extreme, there is a danger of over-regulation by government authorities. In many respects this is exactly what has happened in my own country on the Great Barrier Reef. Bureaucracy (or is it bureaucrazy) seems to have lost touch with reality in its single-minded determination to protect the reef. Protective zoning is implemented over most of the reef, regardless of whether it is needed or not. The bureaucrats mean well and may think they are looking after the best interests of the reef, but they have gone too far. Access to many areas is limited or prohibited, or restrictions on activities such as boating, fishing, reef walking, and snorkelling are enforced. Even though our knowledge of reef biology is still in its infancy, it is nearly impossible for accredited scientists to obtain collection permits, so unbending are the numerous restrictions. One of the most ridiculous edicts I've yet heard was broadcast on television by a government official. He was appealing to visitors on the Great Barrier Reef not to urinate anywhere near corals when swimming. This is all well and good, but how do they intend to stem the flow of urea from the millions of fishes and other marine organisms?

I came across another strange rule during a recent visit to the Caribbean. Underwater photographers were limited to a single flash photo per subject. Heaven forbid the lifelong trauma that multiple flashes might inflict on some unsuspecting coral or fish. Now you may understand why I sometimes question the sanity of our bureaucratic watchdog friends.

I don't think strict law enforcement is the best way to conserve coral reefs, particularly the Great Barrier Reef, which, due to its immense size and great distance from shore, has certain 'built-in' protective devices. I think the real key to the reef's future lies in educating younger generations to respect wildlife rather than exploiting it – in other words, we need to instil strong moral values when it comes to protecting our natural heritage. After all, it's plain commonsense to avoid coral damage, or to catch just enough fish for a few meals, instead of catching 100 at a time. Contrary to what many conservationists preach, it is certainly OK to touch reef animals and plants. This is part and parcel of the reef experience. The basic rule is to always leave things as you find them.

Reef conservationists frequently like to paint a picture of total doom and gloom. They would have us believe that the world's coral reefs are disappearing at a rapid rate, without mentioning the possibility of recovery. Fortunately, reefs are incredibly resistant to all sorts of destructive forces, both man-made and natural. Even the might of the hydrogen bomb has eventually been overcome. Bikini Atoll, site of nuclear tests several decades ago, has dramatically recovered from this awesome devastation. Recolonization by reef organisms can occur virtually overnight, and previously damaged coral communities can be restored within a relatively brief span of time, often fifteen to twenty years or even less. Anyone who has witnessed the spectacular mass spawning of corals, which occurs annually in the Indo-Australian region, will appreciate the enormous regenerative power of coral reefs.

Harmful as it is, the sort of damage inflicted by reef walkers and anchors pales to insignificance compared to lethal natural forces such as cyclones, tidal waves, and earthquakes. In 1990, a group of scientists were conducting a detailed study of an outer reef within the Great Barrier Reef complex. An oncoming cyclone forced them to run for shelter to the mainland. After the eye of the storm had passed 50 kilometres to the north, they returned to an unbelievable scene of devastation. Areas where there had previously been 70 per cent live coral cover were reduced to 5 per cent cover, and even that was damaged. In some places, 2 metres of substrate had simply peeled off and vanished. Extensive damage was also recorded at depths of 40 metres.

Reef systems are also self-destructive through the actions of myriad coral-feeding and boring organisms. Strangely enough, these destructive agents are vital for the continued existence of coral reefs. As explained previously, the limestone or calcium carbonate debris from dead reef animals is eventually 'cemented', forming a solid platform for future coral growth.

Well-meaning conservationists conveniently forget that coral reefs are not permanent fixtures. Like all living things, reefs change with time, sometimes at incredibly rapid rates. They are highly susceptible to the vagaries of weather and other physical phenomena. The situation at Christmas Island and Cocos (Keeling) atoll, Australian territories in the northwest Indian Ocean, is a prime example. For decades these seldom-visited areas were noted for their pristine reefs with abundant coral growth. But in 1983 an El Niño episode

Close-up of brain coral. *Platygyra* sp. (field of view 5 cm), in 5 m, Madang, Papua New Guinea.

caused a rapid worldwide warming of tropical seas by several degrees. This had disastrous effects on living corals, which survive within a fairly narrow temperature range. The lagoon at Cocos was virtually transformed overnight into a foul-smelling mess, resulting from the mass die-off of its corals. Similar wholesale destruction was experienced on the outer fringing reef at neighbouring Christmas Island. Over the ensuing months vast tracts of living coral completely disappeared. The coral dieback precipitated a whole series of environmental changes. One of the most notable was the marked increase in filamentous algal growth, which soon covered the dead coral skeletons. Eventually this caused a pronounced change in the fish community. Coral-feeding species (for example, butterflyfishes), became rare or disappeared, and were replaced by algal feeders, such as surgeonfishes.

A big question mark concerns man's role in shaping our planet's ecology, both below and above the waves. We've all been exposed to the dire warnings of the so-called doomsday ecologists. Global warming has more or less been established as fact, but its possible consequences are open to debate. Although scientists seem unable to offer a precise explanation, there may be a correlation between global warming and a recently discovered phenomenon known as coral bleaching. As this book goes to press, vast quantities of living coral are being destroyed through this process, most notably in parts of Papua New

Coral Grouper with cleanerfish.
Coral Grouper, *Cephalopholis miniatus*
(30 cm); Bicolor Cleanerfish, *Labroides bicolor*,
in 10 m, Great Barrier Reef, Australia.

Guinea. It is caused by the loss of nutrient-giving symbiotic algae that live within the coral tissue and are largely responsible for its colour. As a result, isolated coral formations or entire sections of reef are transformed to a ghostly white. Some corals mysteriously recover, but if the problem persists for more than a few weeks they eventually starve to death.

Any type of reef destruction is sad to witness, but continually changing environmental conditions is one of the factors that makes diving so exciting. It is impossible to predict what to expect at a certain locality from one visit to the next. Marine biologist Jerry Allen and I did a more or less exhaustive survey of Christmas Island fishes in the late 1970s. On subsequent trips, particularly after the El Niño event of 1983, Jerry noted profound changes in the overall reef community. Tulamben, one of my favourite dive sites, situated on the north coast of Bali, provides another good example. The small bay is regularly subjected to storms and periodic upwellings of frigid water from abyssal depths. As a consequence, entire communities of small fishes are regularly extinguished, but are quickly replaced by new communities. It's the most dynamic place I've ever visited. I go there several times every year and the fauna is never the same from one visit to the next.

Zoogeographers have a name for this phenomenon, which accounts for the fact that no two reef areas have exactly the same community of plants and animals. They call it 'sweepstakes dispersal'. Basically this means that the community of organisms found on a particular reef simply reflects what got there first and was able to establish itself. Once the environment has reached saturation, further efforts at colonisation by additional species are usually futile. But this state of affairs does not last very long. For example, if an area is hit by a severe cyclone, entire habitats and the organisms they support can nearly disappear overnight. This opens the door for a new wave of plant and animal colonizers that mix with the remaining survivors. Over eons – years measured in hundreds, thousands, or even hundreds of thousands – and over vast distances such as the entire tropical Indo-Pacific region, the result is a 'patchwork quilt', an endless variety of coral reef communities.

How do colonising organisms reach their final destination? The answer for most tropical marine animals is found in their egg and larval stages. After spawning, the eggs and subsequent larval stages float near the surface and are dispersed by currents. Studies of the growth rings on the otoliths (ear bones) of fishes indicate that the larval stage varies in most species from about one to eight weeks. Therefore the length of the larval stage and pattern of currents are prime factors in determining the distribution of an individual organism. Some species, such as the Longnose Butterflyfish, are incredibly widespread, ranging from East Africa to the Americas. Apparently they are able to use island 'stepping stones' over a number of succeeding generations to spread their gene pool well-beyond distances that correlate with larval duration.

Luxuriant coral growth, Australia.

Corals, mostly *Acropora*, in 5 m,

Lizard Island, Great Barrier Reef, Australia.

The photographic documentation of endemic species has always been one of my high priorities. An endemic is a plant or animal that is confined to a particular place. The scale of endemism may range from tiny individual islands to vast regions such as the Indo-Pacific. Island endemism is particularly fascinating. The number of endemic species is usually related to the degree of isolation, although the actual size of the area is also an important factor. The Hawaiian Islands and Galapagos Archipelago are perhaps the best-known endemic areas and exhibit the highest percentage of unique species (about 20 to 25 per cent). On a larger scale, the Red Sea has a similar percentage.

I'm frequently asked how I became an underwater photographer. Because I grew up in small north Queensland towns (Cairns and Innisfail), this was a slow but very natural progression. For as long as I can remember I've been fascinated with the nearby sea. But the real turning point occurred in my late teens when I was injured in a motorcycle accident. After what at the time seemed an endless period of rehabilitation, further participation in active sports was physically out of the question, but to my pleasant surprise I was completely mobile underwater. This was the beginning of my all-consuming interest in scuba diving.

My interest in the underwater world received a jolt in the early 1970s as a result of a chance meeting with Dr Jerry Allen, a professional ichthyologist, who visited Cairns for several months aboard *El Torito*, a research vessel owned and operated by marine biologist Dr Walt Starck. I was immediately impressed by Jerry's scientific knowledge and powers of observation. It came as a real revelation on our first dive together when he pointed out fishes in my own backyard that I had previously overlooked. He also taught me to pay attention to the smallest details and offered interesting interpretations of behaviour and other aspects of marine life. Ever since, I've welcomed the opportunity to meet and work with marine scientists representing a variety of disciplines.

From these associations, I've learned there is much more to marine academia than meets the eye. It did not take long to break through the facade of microscopes and scientific double-talk to learn that most scientists are real people. In fact, they are some of the most down-to-earth and crazy people I know. They are definitely not the stuffed-shirt, unapproachable stereotypes that the popular media sometimes creates. I've invariably found them helpful, no matter how bothersome my requests for information may be. Nowadays I'm often joined on field trips by my ever-increasing circle of scientific friends. I can't begin to tell you how much I've been able to learn from this interaction, not to mention the fun we have.

I could fill a book with the good times and humorous events that have occurred on trips with scientific colleagues. Two of the best involve Jerry Allen and renowned ichthyologist Dr Jack Randall, former Curator of Fishes at Honolulu's Bishop Museum. Jack is noted for his incredible powers of concentration while diving. Absolutely nothing distracts him once he locks onto a potential fish specimen or photographic subject. With this knowledge, Jerry and I set a little trap for Jack while diving at the Maldives. Female Titan Triggerfish are notoriously aggressive when guarding a nest of eggs. We had both been molested and injured by a particularly savage individual while taking underwater photographs the previous day. At one point Jerry fended an attack by thrusting his camera towards the trigger. The fish actually seized the strobe-mounting bar with its teeth and swam off with the entire camera rig. This was one ferocious fish!

It seems fiendish in retrospect, but somehow seemed entirely appropriate at the time. We hatched a plan whereby we would return to the same spot and line up the triggerfish between Jack and us. Having set this up with ease, we then frantically waved and gestured, indicating we had discovered something extra-exciting to photograph. Jack took the bait and swam in a beeline towards us. Unaware of the trigger, he swam directly above its territory. Boom! The fish erupted like a heat-seeking missile. I've never seen anyone swim as fast as Jack, with the trigger in hot pursuit and biting at every opportunity.

The second incident occurred in the Solomon Islands. Jerry was photographing and Jack was collecting specimens with a Hawaiian-sling spear. These pursuits do not always mix, as I learned from the hilarious scene that unfolded. Jack was moving at top speed in mad pursuit of a small rudderfish. At last he lined up a shot and drew back the firing rubber. His concentration was so intense that he did not see Jerry, who was positioned several metres away, directly behind the target. He launched the spear, missed the veering fish, and shot Jerry squarely in the butt! Fortunately Jerry was wearing a thick wetsuit and was far enough away for the shot to have lost most of its impetus. These 'scientific' moments are sacred to me. Funny you never hear or read about them at international symposia or in scholarly journals.

Male fairy basslet.

Pseudanthias bimaculatus (12 cm), in 35 m, Tulamben, Bali, Indonesia.

I should tell you more about Jack Randall. He's certainly one of the most amazing people I've ever met. At seventy-three years of age, Jack is considered a living legend among his ichthyological colleagues. He is universally acknowledged as the 'guru' of coral-reef fish knowledge. The energy of this man, be it in the laboratory or out in the field, is absolutely astounding. Jack has written more than 400 scientific papers and numerous books. He has described hundreds of new fish species over a career that spans nearly fifty years. You might think at his age he would be contemplating retirement or at least think of slowing down a notch or two. Not Jack. I recently joined him on a visit to northern Sulawesi. He managed a total of thirteen dives on the last two days – I counted them.

Jerry Allen was one of Jack's first PhD students at the University of Hawaii, back in the late 1960s An eminent authority in his own right, Jerry credits Jack as the motivating force in his career.

'I'm sure if it were not for Jack, I would not have chosen coral reef fishes as my life's work – probably would have ended up as a shoe salesman at K-Mart,' he relates.

Dr Walter Starck is another scientist who has played a profound role in stimulating my marine biological interests. I've had countless wonderful opportunities aboard his research vessel *El Torito*. It was a sad day when Walt eventually retired the boat. But I still enjoy frequently swapping stories with him. He lives about two hours north of Cairns, alongside the picturesque Daintree River. Walt is definitely one of the most interesting people I know.

At an age when most of us mere mortals only dream about sailing around the South Seas, Walt put his dream into action. Just out of college and short of cash, he boldly walked into a New Orleans shipbuilding firm and placed an order for *El Torito*. This done, he figured out a way to pay for the vessel – by selling a package of one-hour TV specials to a big American network. About a year later he was cruising with his wife and two young children through the Panama Canal on his way to Pacific in his new boat. *El Torito* was specifically designed for comfort and to serve as a tool for marine biological research. The mini-ship was only 20 metres long, but exceptionally beamy, with a width of nearly 10 metres. Below decks the spacious airconditioned quarters included three staterooms, a laboratory-library, dining salon, kitchen, and engine room. Underwater activities were well-catered for with an array of scuba tanks including mixed gas rebreathers, two air compressors, a decompression chamber, underwater still and movie cameras with a closed-circuit video link, and a two-person wet submarine.

With a top speed of only 8 knots, progress was slow but steady. Walt's first destination in the Pacific was Hawaii. After a short stop he cruised westward to the islands of Micronesia. This was towards the end of 1971. He eventually arrived at Palau, where Jerry Allen was working. A few months later, when he headed south for New Guinea and Australia, Jerry was aboard with his wife Connie and young son. Cairns was the first port of call in Australia. The vessel's unusual shape and the bright yellow submarine sitting on deck caught my eye one afternoon as I motored by in my dinghy after checking crab pots in Admiralty Inlet. I came aboard for a chat and Jerry gave me a tour. Although Walt was in Sydney at the time, we fast became friends when he returned.

Walt has an incredible knowledge of marine biology, and as far as technical gadgets and do-it-yourself workmanship are concerned, he's the closest thing to a genius I've come across. He received his PhD from the University of Miami at the tender age of twenty-two. During his university days he earned spare cash by inventing and

Soft coral archway, Fiji.
Soft corals, mostly *Dendronephthya*, in 15 m, Taveuni, Fiji.

selling the Slurpgun (a device for catching small aquarium fishes) and the better-known Bangstick (a type of shark protection consisting of a modified Hawaiian-sling spear with a screw-tip powerhead for firing shotgun shells). He also co-invented the Electrolung, the first commercially manufactured rebreather for deep diving.

I have lots of Walt stories. He's a great guy with a remarkably sharp wit, who loves a practical joke. I have this obsessive thing about cockroaches – just can't stand them. Prior to one of our regular trips out to the Barrier Reef I even paid a professional exterminator to spray the boat. On the first day of the

Aeolid sea slug.

Cuthona sp. (4 cm), in 3 m,

Tulamben, Bali, Indonesia.

cruise we were having lunch around the salon table. I was enjoying a coke and as I tipped the glass to drain it I suddenly turned a shade of green and bolted for the toilet. There was a huge dead cockroach in the bottom of my glass! Of course it was a rubber one that Walt had carefully planted.

Another not so famous trait is Walt's notorious impatience. Everyone aboard *El Torito* has experienced it in some shape or form. Walt definitely works to his own schedule, and has the rather unpleasant habit of pulling up the anchor and departing when least expected. Jerry and I have been caught in mid-dive on several occasions. One morning near Lizard Island on the Barrier Reef, we were working from a small rubber dingy. Next thing we knew Walt was steaming south. It took us over an hour to catch the boat and he refused to stop, even when we finally came alongside. Of course Walt thought this was a good joke. The worst incident of this ilk transpired in the Solomon Islands. I wasn't aboard, but Jerry Allen related his nightmare experience to me. They had been anchored three days at the same site on a totally submerged reef about 15 kilometres off the island of Malaita. Jerry was scuba diving down the steep dropoff directly below the boat. When he surfaced, *El Torito* was a mere dot on the horizon. Surprise! Walt had suddenly pulled anchor and departed. Several hours later, when everyone sat down for lunch, Walt realised someone was missing. Fortunately, the story had a happy ending. Jerry ditched his scuba gear and trod water until the boat finally returned. As the *El Torito* approached, Walt grinned and shouted, 'Did you enjoy the dive?'

Through my association with Walt, Jack and Jerry, I've learned to appreciate the highly exciting process of discovering and describing new species. It fascinates me to think that new botanical and zoological discoveries still abound in this fast-paced age of ultra-computer technology and exploration of outer space. The advent of scuba diving in the 1940s sparked a new exciting era of underwater exploration. Scientists could now submerge for extended periods while searching for new and unusual organisms. In the case of marine fishes, this process was greatly accelerated by the use of chemical ichthyocides, which drive even the most secretive species from cover. This golden age of discovery is still in full swing. Jerry Allen estimates that he and diving colleagues such as Jack Randall collectively discover twenty to thirty new species of tropical marine fishes each year. The wealth of new invertebrates is even more impressive. I've attempted to give readers a glimpse of this fascinating world of discovery by featuring photographs of at least sixteen as yet unnamed species in this book.

And there's no end in sight – thanks to modern deep-diving technology. Richard Pyle, a PhD student at the University of Hawaii, working under Jack Randall's tutelage, is on the cutting edge of this new wave of discovery. He is perfecting techniques of collecting fishes and other marine organisms with the use of sophisticated rebreather scuba gear. On a recent visit to Milne Bay, Papua New Guinea, Richard and fellow deep-diver John Earle collected twenty new species while diving at depths in excess of 122 metres (400 feet).

Although my efforts pale in comparison to those of the elite band of diving scientists, it is most gratifying to have played at least a small part in the discovery process. On several occasions my underwater photographs of previously undetected fishes and invertebrates have alerted scientists to the existence of these animals. Several scientific colleagues have graciously invited me to join them in authoring descriptions of new species, and they have even named several *steenei*. This is the ultimate buzz for an underwater photographer!

One of the things I like best about diving is that no two dives, even when made at the same place, are ever the same. Each dive presents a unique learning experience, and the behavioural interactions of the plants and animals one encounters are totally unpredictable. In my first coffee-table book, *Coral Reefs: Nature's Richest Realm*, I invited readers to send me accounts of any interesting or unusual observations of their own. I received hundreds of replies. One of the most interesting was from a lady in Hong Kong who related the following observations: 'My partner and I were confronted by a large cuttlefish, which performed an incredible colour-flashing display while hovering directly in front of us. It seemed it was trying to attract our attention, almost as though it wanted us to follow. That's exactly what we did for a distance of about 50 metres. It finally lead us to a fish trap where a struggling cuttlefish was tethered as bait. We gently released the animal, which sparked another display of spectacular colours. I guess this was a sort of thank you message. They then swiftly departed.'

Another favourite story was related to me by Max Benjamin, owner of Walindi Plantation Resort on the Papua New Guinea island of New Britain. A group of divers from the resort encountered a whale shark on a distant pinnacle reef. It had somehow managed to tightly entwine its body in a collar of thick rope, which was cutting into the animal's flesh and obviously causing it a great deal of distress. The dive boat sent an SOS to Max. It took him more than an hour to arrive at the site, but the whale shark was still there. Max and another diver went down with sturdy knives to cut away the rope. Incredibly the ponderous animal responded as though it knew help was imminent. Although it had been continually swimming for the previous two hours, it suddenly stopped and stood perfectly still, dropping tail-first to a depth of 35 metres, as the divers methodically removed its rope shackle.

I think both of these encounters indicate that marine animals, particularly cephalopods and vertebrates, are more intelligent than we often give them credit for. Once again I encourage readers to share any interesting stories or photographs based on their own observations of unusual behaviour involving marine subjects. Please refer to the 'Photographic Details' section at the end of this book.

Filamentous Flasher Wrasse.

Paracheilinus filamentosus (5 cm), in 20 m,

Russell Islands, Solomon Islands.

I'm often asked to name the most difficult subject I've ever photographed. The answer is easy. Without a doubt it's the Filamentous Flasher Wrasse (*Paracheilinus filamentosus*), a particularly elegant, small (about 5 centimetres) fish that inhabits reefs of Indonesia and Melanesia. To me this fish represents the ultimate challenge, the supreme test of a photographer's ability. Actually, it's not that difficult to photograph. The real challenge is to capture a courting male with fins fully erect, as it momentarily flashes luminous courtship colours and performs a jerky ritualistic dance. So far I've accumulated twenty hours in pursuit of the perfect photo of this majestic animal, but have yet to succeed.

Another question I'm often asked: 'Is diving dangerous and have you had any close calls?' Diving is usually as safe as you choose to make it. Fortunately, I haven't had any problems, but I pride myself in not taking chances and making sure that my equipment is always in good working order. Of course there are certain dangers in almost everything we do, even crossing the street. But to be totally honest, the potential dangers of diving never enter my mind. The only thing I think about during a dive is locating a good photographic subject. Once I'm 'locked in' it's a matter of total concentration. It may take hours of repeated dives on the same subject until I'm happy with the results.

Although I've been lucky in keeping out of trouble, some of my friends' hair-raising experiences serve as a reminder that accidents are not always avoidable. In March 1996, as this book was being prepared, Dr Tony Ayling, a marine biologist friend, was attacked by a 3.5-metre crocodile while scuba diving on a fringing reef off Queensland's Cape York Peninsula.

The attack took place on a murky coastal reef while Tony was conducting a routine biological survey. Visibility was reduced to about a metre and he did not see the crocodile approach. Even when it seized him by the foot, a crocodile was the last thing he thought of. A Giant Grouper would have been a far more likely attacker, and at first this is what Tony thought had him by the foot. But the animal suddenly jackknifed, swinging Tony close into its body, leaving no doubt about the attacker's identity. A life-and-death struggle ensued. The croc clung tenaciously to Tony's foot, violently writhing in an attempt to gain

Colonial anemones on sea whip.

Amphianthus sp. (3 cm), in 18 m,

Lembeh Straits, Sulawesi, Indonesia.

a death grip. At the same time, Tony clawed at the croc's eyes, pounded it on the head with a metallic tape measure, and pounded its body with his fists. The struggle continued for several minutes, with the croc eventually towing Tony to the surface and then back to the bottom. Thankfully, he was still connected to his scuba gear, otherwise he would have surely drowned. In a last-ditch effort, he seized one of the croc's front legs with both his hands and levered it upwards. The croc suddenly released its grip and swam off into the gloom. Tony had miraculously survived, having sustained only a badly crushed foot that required surgery, not to mention the fright of his life.

Dr Ayling must consider himself a very lucky man. Not so lucky were the four victims of Tiger Shark attacks at Madang, Papua New Guinea, which took place only a couple of weeks before Tony's incident. This is one of the most bizarre tales I've encountered. Madang is one my favourite dive spots. I've spent hundreds of hours in the water there over the past three decades, and have seen very few sharks, none of them Tigers. I was therefore amazed to hear about the events that unfolded in February 1996.

Three young men were attacked in three separate incidents in the same place, all on the same day – 7 February. Two of the victims died horrible deaths, resulting from loss of limbs. The third, a student, miraculously survived despite being bitten. Aside from the lack of previous attacks in the area, the really strange thing about this incident is that the second and third attacks were even allowed to happen, not to mention a fourth and yet another fatal attack, which occurred ten days later. It seems there was little or no attempt to warn anyone about what was happening. Madang is a large town with a reasonably well-staffed police department – so why wasn't an immediate warning sounded?

The first three victims were swimming at the surface. At least two of them were spearfishing. The fourth, Elijah Sapi, suffered fatal wounds in a terrifying encounter only metres from his son. He was mauled at 6.30 a.m. while fishing from a rock in waist-deep water, just a short distance from where the previous encounters occurred. The four attacks can most likely be attributed to the same shark, perhaps an old or injured 'rogue', no longer able to capture its normal prey. An all-out fishing assault was finally launched after the death of the final victim. A supply of oversized shark hooks was specially flown in from Australia. Eventually a 4-metre Tiger was caught and the attacks ceased. The shark was hung by its tail from a limb of a mango tree and, according to the local newspaper, attracted a crowd of more than 5000 people.

Then there's always the possibility of natural disasters. A tidal wave would be the farthest thing from my mind while diving, but they do happen, particularly in Southeast Asia, where earthquakes and volcanic eruptions are common. Maumere Bay, on the Indonesian island of Flores, is another one of my favourite dive locations. Six months after my most recent visit this beautiful site was swept by a freak earthquake-generated tidal wave. The consequences were terrible – about 1200 lives lost (mostly on one small island I've often dived at) and vast areas of reef totally destroyed. Some of the fringing reefs there simply broke off their volcanic-cone base and slid into the unknown.

Most of the photos that appear in this book were taken over the past five years. Ironically, those that represent the smallest part of my overall portfolio are the ones that take the most time. I'm referring to wide-angle shots that bisect the sea's surface, with the submerged reef featured in the bottom half and the surface landscape in the upper half. The act of shooting 'half-ins' is not all that difficult, but setting up these photos is a real nightmare. It usually takes a day or two to find suitable sites where rich corals abound in exceptionally shallow water next to shore and there is an interesting surface landscape. Then comes the really difficult part – getting the weather to cooperate. The shots can only be taken in brilliant sunlight when seas are glassy smooth. On an average trip of three to four weeks, these conditions might exist for a total of thirty to forty minutes – if I'm lucky. When it happens, it's a mad rush to reach the preselected shooting site before the wind picks up or clouds obscure the sun. It's a frustrating game, but I love it. These same trials and tribulations apply to getting good underwater reflection shots, which show the reefs details perfectly mirrored on the surface.

Another labour-intensive technique involves the use of a special Optical Bench with ultra-high magnification capabilities. This highly technical device was designed by Peter Parks of Image Quest – 3D, in London. Whenever Peter visits the Lizard Island Research Station on the Great Barrier Reef, I try to take advantage of this equipment.

Unusual sponge forms.
Pericharax sp. (4 cm), in 8 m,
Walindi, Papua New Guinea.

Garden of invertebrates.

Mixed invertebrates, unidentified

(field of view 30 cm), in 15 m,

Tolandono, Tukang Besi, Indonesia.

It takes long hours to set up, but the results are more than worthwhile. Thanks to Peter's technology, I've become aware of an incredible world of microscopic organisms that are just as interesting and diverse as the reef's larger inhabitants. It's a real pleasure to share this unseen world with readers.

What do I like best about my life as an underwater photographer? It's a combination of meeting lots of interesting people and constantly travelling to exotic locations. Diving seems to get easier with each passing year – thanks to the booming travel industry. There are more flights to more exotic destinations than ever before. There has been a concurrent blossoming of dive facilities. On a recent visit to Sharm-el-Sheikh on the Red Sea, I counted more than 200 commercial dive boats. The Maldives is another example of an area where dive tourism has literally exploded. There are now more than seventy hotels offering underwater services. This is a far cry from the 1960s, when we had to carry our own compressor and tanks on most dive trips.

I've already mentioned the ultra-deep diving exploits of Richard Pyle. It may be true that a large majority of recent fish discoveries have occurred below 30 metres, but for my money, life is much more pleasant in the shallows. I've long noticed this deep-diving machismo thing that prevails in diving circles. Basically it equates to 'deeper is better'. Nothing could be further from the truth. I've done my share of 50-metre dives, and can honestly say they are less productive than shallow-water experiences. It's well-known that corals and the myriad life forms that are associated with reefs thrive where light conditions are optimal. Biodiversity diminishes rapidly with increasing depth. Below 20 to 30 metres from the surface, most of the light spectra necessary for coral growth are filtered out. Consequently, this environment supports a paucity of life compared to the sunlit shallows. Another consideration is the amount of time one can spend while submerged. On standard single-tank scuba dives, bottom time is reduced to a few precious minutes each day at depths below 30 metres, compared to hours of bottom time at depths of less than 10 metres. The extraordinary wealth of marine life coupled with almost unlimited bottom time explains why I'm proud to be a shallow-water diver.

One of the biggest rewards from my photographic endeavours is being invited to check out new dive facilities. In recent years some of my best trips have been to highly efficient dive resorts or on live-aboard boats at New Britain, Borneo, or the Indonesian islands of Java, Kalimantan, Bali, Komodo, Flores, Ambon, and Sulawesi.

As you can see, Indonesia features prominently in the above list of dive sites. It is without doubt my favourite destination. Also, it's no coincidence that Indonesia just happens to be directly in the middle of the world's richest biological province. More than one-third of all marine fish species reside in the archipelago and the figure for invertebrates is equally impressive. It's a tremendously exciting area that is just starting to develop as far as diving facilities and access are concerned. The Indonesian Archipelago stretches for over 5000 kilometres and contains more than 13 667 individual islands. Imagine the endless possibilities for photography. No two islands are ever the same. I've barely scratched the surface at just a few of the better-known sites. Any serious-minded underwater photographer not currently working in Indonesia is going backwards.

One final word regarding the major aim of this book. It's not intended to be educational, but if you manage to learn something about the sea's incredible diversity and its strange ways of life, so much the better. There's no sublime message here, or preaching of a personal philosophy (I get a kick out of authors who carry on about their surreal experiences and ability to commune with nature every time they slip below the waves). There's nothing like that in these pages. You may have guessed it already – the motivating factor for all of my diving and photography is simple enjoyment. A profound appreciation of the amazing natural world is extra reward. Basically this is the message contained in these pages – enjoyment of nature's richest realm and an appreciation of the coral reef's endless living treasures. Accumulating the photos that fill these pages has been fun and extremely rewarding. I'm happy to share them with readers and sincerely hope you enjoy this true labour of love.

Clownfish family with anemone.
Clownfish, *Amphiprion percula* (5 cm);
anemone, *Heteractis magnifica*, in 5 m,
Walindi, Papua New Guinea.

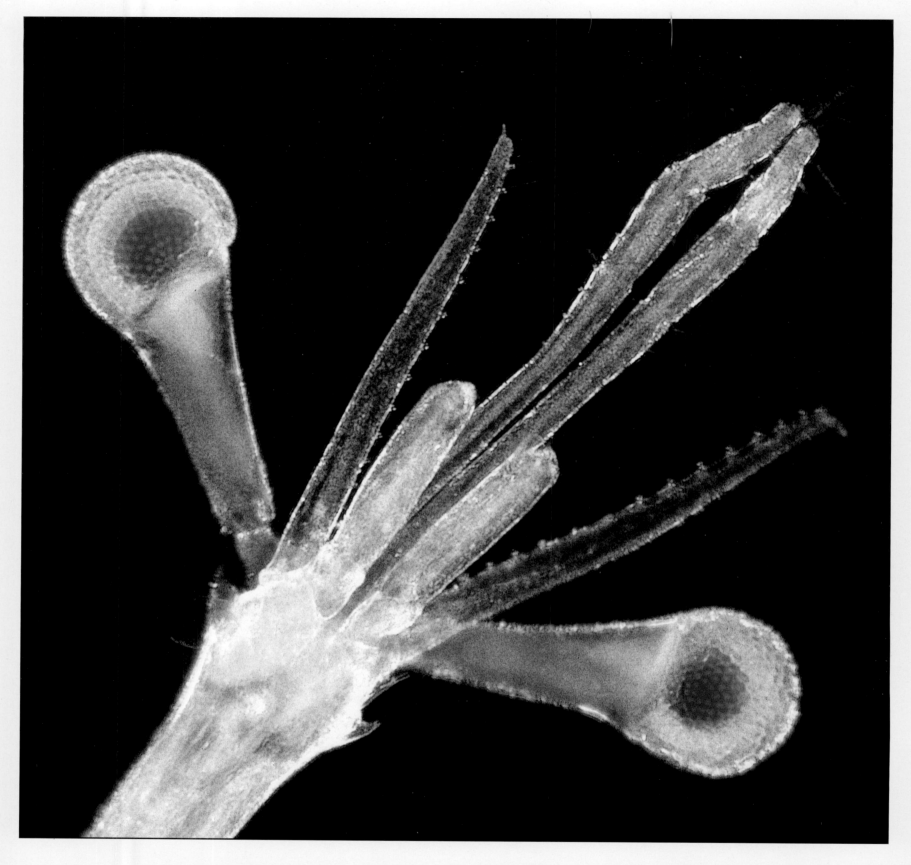

The head of this larval crustacean is dominated by feeding appendages and prominent eyestalks. Crustaceans typically possess compound eyes, composed of numerous separate visual units. Each has its own lens and photoreceptor cells.

Lucifer sp. (8 mm), Lizard Island, Great Barrier Reef, Australia.

Opposite: Rivalling a spectacular fireworks display, chondrophoran siphonophores aggregate on the surface in still conditions. They were previously thought to be a colony of hydrozoan polyps, but are now believed to be a highly modified single hydroid polyp.

Drifting Siphonophores, *Porpita* sp. (1-3 cm), Lizard Island, Great Barrier Reef, Australia.

Sweetlips are known for their dramatic colour transformations
from the juvenile to adult stage. When they are mature, this
vivid pattern dissolves into an unremarkable coat of dark spots.

Many-spotted Sweetlips, *Plectorhinchus chaetodontoides* (10 cm), in 5 m, Manado, Sulawesi, Indonesia.

The juvenile Barramundi Cod is one of the reef's most spectacular inhabitants.
It swims as though it is having buoyancy problems. The head is angled downward,
while the body and pectoral fins are waved vigorously from side to side.

Cromileptes altivelis (9 cm), in 23 m, Lembeh Straits, Sulawesi, Indonesia.

Every nook and cranny on the reef is a potential home. The Red-spotted Blenny is
partial to abandoned worm tubes. It makes quick forays into the open to feed on algae.

Istiblennius chrysospilos (5 cm), in 2 m, Tulamben, Bali, Indonesia.

Maternal instincts are strong, even in the sea. A gravid Harlequin Crab assumes an
aggressive stance with claws bared. It protects the clearly evident yellow egg mass
under the belly. This species usually associates with sand anemones.

Lissocarcinus laevis (8 cm), in 6 m, Lembeh Straits, Sulawesi, Indonesia.

This tiny mollusc scavenges the bottom, 'tasting' the
surrounding waters with its extended siphon. It crawls over
any obstacle in its path, in this instance the arm of a starfish.

Mosaic Starfish, *Fromia monilis*; unidentified mollusc (8 mm), in 5 m, Lembeh Straits, Sulawesi, Indonesia

Trapeze crabs live symbiotically with hard corals, scuttling among the branches.
Usually a small male and large female share the same colony.
This female is carrying eggs under the protective flap of her abdomen.

Red-spotted Trapeze Crab, *Trapezia rufopunctata* (5 cm), in 5 m, Tulamben, Bali, Indonesia.

When disturbed, the spectacular Comet retreats head first, exposing its rear half.
In this position it is an effective mimic of the Spotted Moray Eel, the gap
between the lower fins resembling the mouth with a false eyespot above.

Calloplesiops altivelis (13 cm), in 3 m, Manado, Sulawesi, Indonesia.

Unique among marine fishes, males of the Banggai Cardinalfish brood
both eggs and young in their mouth. After a few weeks the babies
abandon this protection and seek permanent refuge in nearby sea urchins.

Pterapogon kauderni (7cm), in 2 m, Banggai Island, Sulawesi, Indonesia.

Wonderpuss the Octopus

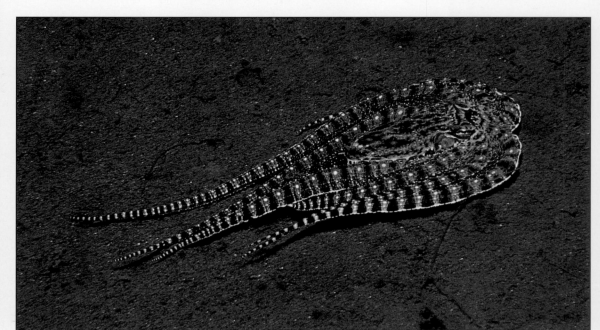
As itself

As a flounder

As a sand anemone

As a stingray

As a lionfish

As a baby cuttlefish

As a jawfish

As a snake eel

As a brittlestar

As a jellyfish

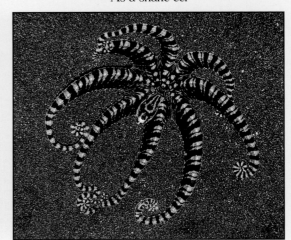
As a featherstar

As a sea snake

The recently discovered but still unnamed Mimic Octopus is a master of disguise. It lives on sandy bottoms, assuming the shapes of a diverse range of animals. In addition to those shown here, it also mimics a hermit crab, a nudibranch, a seahorse, and a mantis shrimp. Its deception is further enhanced by copying the exact movements of the mimicked subjects.

Octopus sp. (60 cm), in 4 m, Maumere, Flores, and Lembeh Straits, Sulawesi, Indonesia ('jellyfish' photo by Denise Nielsen-Tackett).

As something unrecognisable

The Bobbit worm unfolds gargantuan jaws, a spring-loaded trap lethal to any passing fish. Unique in the animal kingdom, its massive jaw structure is twice the body width. Growing to 3 metres, this voracious predator is active at night and known to attack divers.

Eunicid polychaete (jaw width 2.5 cm), in 2 m, Anilao, Philippines.

Ascidians are sensitive to the slightest touch, closing their siphons in an instant.
These animals have obviously spent their lives in close proximity,
and the ascidian tolerates the crab's presence.

Galatheid crab, galatheid sp. (1 cm); Yellow Ascidian, *Phallusia julinea*, in 22 m, Madang, Papua New Guinea.

Opposite: The Bubble Shell resembles an ordinary seashell, but is actually closely
related to nudibranchs. Its delicate shell is easily crushed if handled roughly. The ruffled
skirt-like mantle, completely retractable in most shells, is always partly exposed.

Hydatina physis (8 cm), in 3 m, Lembeh Straits, Sulawesi, Indonesia.

The Umbrella Crab is aptly named. It has the unusual habit of shielding its upper
surface with a sponge or other reef organisms, in this case a piece of gorgonian.
The last two pairs of legs have claws used to carry the 'umbrella'.

Dromidiopsis edwardsi (18 cm), in 8 m, Tulamben, Bali, Indonesia.

The young of this fish is bright red with large white spots, and appropriately
the species is known as the Clown Wrasse. In contrast, the adult male,
shown here, has a completely different pattern. It is capable of
turning over surprisingly large stones in search of food.

Coris gaimard (25 cm), in 3 m, Tulamben, Bali, Indonesia.

The Spiny Leaf Fish, a member of the scorpionfish family, takes it name
from an unusual type of mimicry. When threatened it gently rocks
from side to side, appearing remarkably similar to a drifting leaf.

Ablabys macracanthus (12 cm), in 6 m, Maumere, Flores, Indonesia.

Opposite: Spider crabs use their claws to camouflage themselves by
attaching algae, sponges, and hydroids. The individual featured here
has protected itself with hairy tufts, actually the stinging polyps of a hydroid.

Unidentified spider crab, majid (2 cm); unidentified blue tunicate, in 20 m, Komodo Island, Indonesia.

Coral reef organisms exhibit marked depth zonation. This phenomenon is most
apparent on the edge of dropoffs. Very different communities inhabit the wave-swept
shallows, compared to those found in the shaded crevices and fissures of steep slopes.

Ras Za'atir, Sharm-el-Sheikh, Red Sea, Egypt.

Schools of small plankton-feeding basslets and damselfishes erupt in a
synchronised explosion of flashing colour when they emerge from their coral sanctuary
to feed in the water column. They return to the coral in unison when alarmed.

Fairy Basslets, *Pseudanthias squamipinnis* (each 6 cm); mixed damselfishes, pomacentrids, in 12 m,

Sharm-el-Sheikh, Red Sea, Egypt.

The behaviour of reef fishes is variable depending on geographic locality.
The Coronation Trout is wary and difficult to approach at most places,
but the opposite is true in the Red Sea.

Variola louti (50 cm), in 18 m, Sharm-el-Sheikh, Red Sea, Egypt.

The highly flamboyant reef lobsters belonging to the genus *Enoplometopus*
occur widely on Indo-Pacific coral reefs. Unlike their plate-sized mouth-watering
relatives, they only reach a maximum length of about 20 centimetres.

Ornate Reef Lobster, *Enoplometopus holthuisi* (10 cm), in 15 m, Madang, Papua New Guinea.

Premnas biaculeatus differs from the other 27 types of anemonefishes in having
a prominent backward-projecting spine on the cheek. Females grow much larger
than males. This individual, 15 centimetres in length, is one of the largest ever recorded.

Spine-cheek Anemonefish, *Premnas biaculeatus*, in 2 m, Lembeh Straits, Manado, Indonesia.

When suddenly disturbed the Flame File Shell scuttles away with a
jerky movement, rapidly opening and shutting its valves to force out a jet of water.
The extremely sticky tentacles are used defensively to deter predatory fishes.

Lima sp. (4 cm), in 12 m, Manado, Sulawesi, Indonesia.

The Thin-spined Rockcod differs from most other groupers in having separate juvenile
and adult colours. This young individual will soon undergo a remarkable transformation.
When the change is complete, this bright pattern will be replaced by dull shades of grey.

Gracila albomarginata (15 cm), in 8 m, Walindi, Papua New Guinea.

An almost endless range of vivid colours is displayed by the spiky soft corals
(*Dendronephthya*). Is there a single variable species or are there many, each
represented by different shapes and colours? This question remains unanswered.

Dendronephthya sp. (colony 120 cm), in 18 m, Taveuni, Fiji.

Trapeze crabs are easily recognized by their distinctive carapace shape
and prominent clawed legs. This dwarf species is brooding a
clutch of eggs while nestling among the polyps of a stony coral.
Red Trapeze Crab, *Quadrella boopsis* (2 cm), in 15 m, Kunkungan Bay, Sulawesi, Indonesia.

Opposite: Spider crabs are remarkably diverse in size and shape.
They range from the gigantic Japanese Spider Crab, with metre-long legs,
to the miniature coral-reef species seen here. Their patterns blend
remarkably well with the polyp-studded texture of their hosts.
Above: *Xenocarcinus conicus* (1.5 cm), in 18 m, Tulamben, Bali, Indonesia.
Below: *Xenocarcinus tuberculatus* (1.5 cm), in 15 m, Lembeh Straits, Sulawesi, Indonesia.

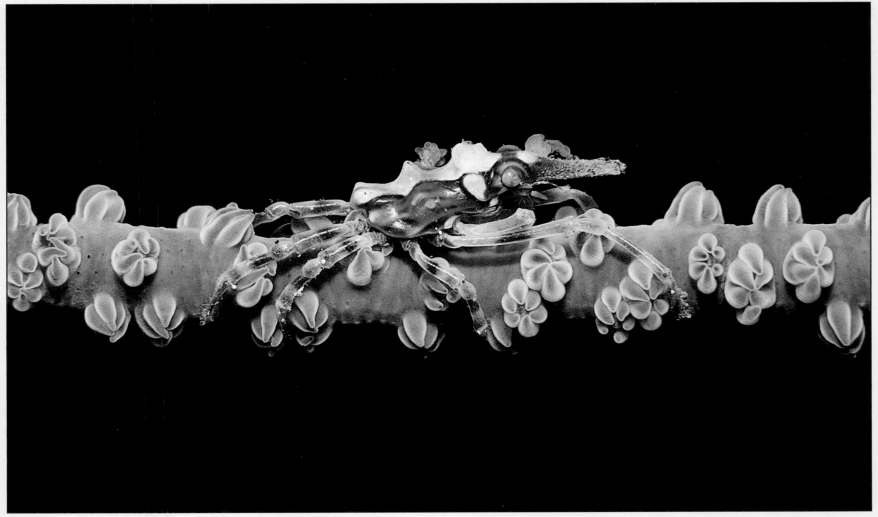

This rare Rock Porcelain Crab was discovered just in time for
inclusion in the book. Like other porcelain crabs, it is a filter feeder,
using its mouthpart appendages to sieve food items.

Petrolisthes sp. (3 cm), in 2 m, Tulamben, Bali, Indonesia.

Opposite: Ladybug Amphipods swarm onto the surface of soft corals
to feed on detritus. They periodically regroup after swimming to
another coral colony. The photographed species is probably new to science.

Cyproidea sp. (each 3 mm), in 15 m, Komodo, Indonesia.

The unusual pattern of the Clown Triggerfish presents
a classic example of disruptive colouration. Its markings
effectively break up the body outline, confusing potential attackers.

Balistoides conspicillum (22 cm), in 10 m, Walindi, Papua New Guinea.

Low spring tides occasionally expose impressive stands of living coral. The most
expansive growths can be seen on Australia's relatively inaccessible Great Barrier Reef.
Unfortunately, corals are damaged in many other areas by reef walkers gathering food.

Flynn Reef, Cairns, Australia.

A spiky soft coral is the entire universe for the diminutive Candy-striped Cowry.
This photograph was taken as eggs were being deposited
on the host's spicule-impregnated stalk.

Serratovolva dondani (1 cm), in 18 m, Tulamben, Bali, Indonesia.

Opposite: Hermit crabs begin life as planktonic larvae. After a series of moults,
they transform into small adults and settle out on a reef. Survival then depends on
finding a suitable coat of armour in the form of an abandoned mollusc shell.

Unidentified larval hermit crab (3 mm), Lizard Island, Great Barrier Reef, Australia.

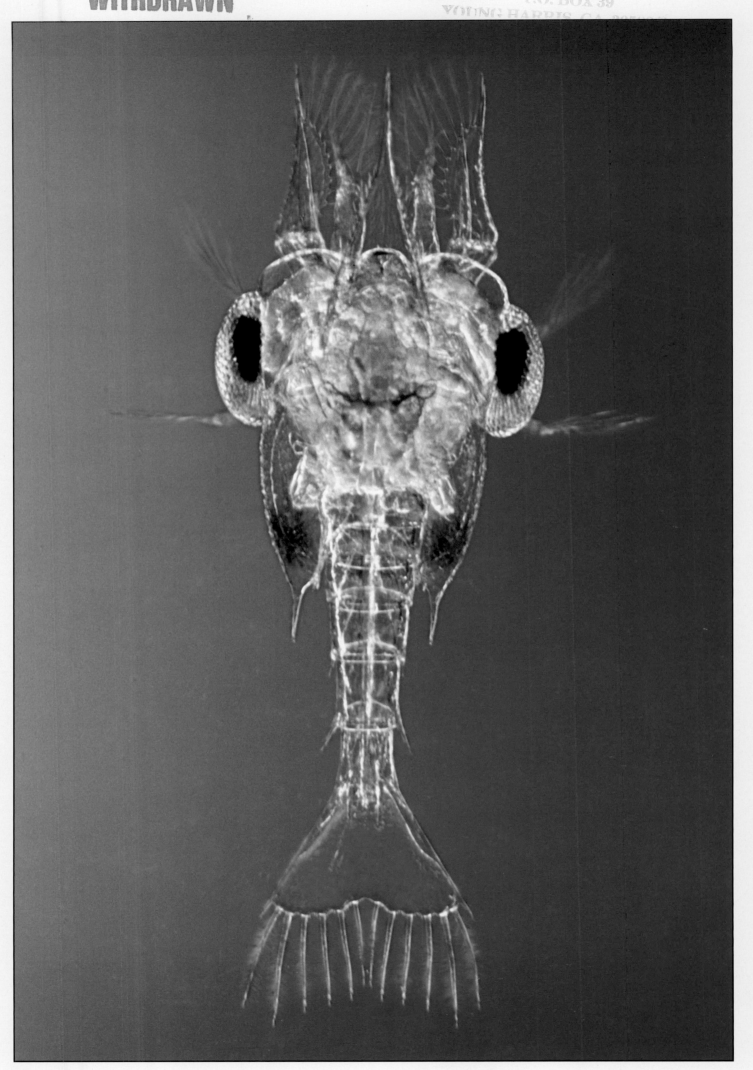

The Candy Crab is the ultimate camouflage artist, being virtually invisible in its natural surroundings. It trims small branches off its host soft coral, carefully attaching them to the spines on the top of its head. Amazingly, the polyps continue to flourish.

Hoplophrys oatesii (1.5 cm), in 20 m, Tulamben, Bali, Indonesia.

The transparent alima larva of a stomatopod crustacean appears far less menacing
than a mature mantis shrimp, into which it eventually transforms.

Unidentified larval stomatopod (5 mm), Lizard Island, Great Barrier Reef, Australia.

It's not unusual to encounter sea cucumbers massed together. Possibly they congregate for mating, or simply attracted to prominent outcrops on the reef for plankton feeding.

Yellow Sea Cucumber, *Pentacta lutea* (5 cm), in 18 m, Komodo Island, Indonesia.

Unlike its relatives, the hermit crab avoids periods of high vulnerability
when undergoing the moulting process. It simply finds a new,
larger shell to accommodate its increased body size.

Scarlet Hermit Crab, *Dardanus megistos* (12 cm), in 3 m, Sandfly Passage, Solomon Islands.

Opposite: Bright colours, strange eyes, and peculiar behaviour make the
Rainbow Mantis Shrimp the clown of the reef. This individual was
photographed in an unusual pose, with its tail curled underneath its head.

Odontodactylus scyllarus (10 cm), in 20 m, Tulamben, Bali, Indonesia.

Relatively few fishes exhibit the unusual habit of oral egg incubation.
The eggs of this jawfish are clearly visible in this photograph.
After hatching, the young lead a pelagic existence for several weeks.

Randall's Jawfish, *Opistognathus* sp. (10 cm), in 4 m, Ambon, Indonesia.

Opposite: Growing to 20 centimetres, the Fingered Dragonet has excellent camouflage
that blends well with the bottom until the large, colourful fins are displayed. Its name is
derived from the finger-like ventral-fin rays, which are used for crawling.

Dactylopus dactylopus. Above: Juvenile (5 cm), in 4 m, Gilimanuk, Bali, Indonesia.

Below: Adult (15 cm), in 8 m, Lembeh Straits, Sulawesi, Indonesia.

The peculiar disc on the head of the Suckerfish enables this
seagoing hitchhiker to attach to large marine animals.
They eat scraps produced by the feeding activities of their host.
Slender Suckerfish, *Echeneis naucrates* (60 cm), in 15 m, Tulamben, Bali, Indonesia.

Previous pages: Gobies are the most abundant family of fishes found
on coral reefs. They exhibit a wide range of colours and markings, but due
to their small size and inconspicuous habits, their beauty is seldom noticed.
Above left: Wheeler's Shrimp Goby, *Amblyeleotris wheeleri* (5 cm), in 10 m, Tulamben, Bali, Indonesia.
Below left: Orange-spotted Goby, *Coryphopterus longispinus* (5 cm), in 12 m, Tulamben, Bali, Indonesia.
Above right: Orange-dashed Goby, *Valenciennea puellaris* (10 cm), in 12 m, Tulamben, Bali, Indonesia.
Below right: Metallic Shrimp Goby, *Amblyeleotris latifasciata* (10 cm), in 18 m, Tulamben, Bali, Indonesia.

The subtle yet distinctive colours of parrotfishes are useful for recognizing
the estimated 80 species. The family is renowned for sex reversal,
characterized by drab juveniles and females transforming to gaudy males.

Surf Parrotfish, *Scarus rivulatus* (40 cm), in 12 m, Russell Islands, Solomon Islands.

Massive anchovy schools form along the west Australian coast
during winter calms. Lasting up to several weeks, each precipitates
a wild feeding frenzy by whales, sharks, and predatory fishes.

Anchovy school, Cape Cuvier, Western Australia.

Opposite: Barrier reefs develop on the edge of a continental shelf
in a process similar to atoll formation. This mosaic of shallow corals
was photographed on Queenland's famous Great Barrier Reef.

Elford Reef, Australia.

This ever-alert anemone crab presents deceivingly large nippers
to discourage its enemies. However, these weapons are
actually wafer thin despite their formidable appearance.

Porcelain crab, *Neopetrolisthes ohshimai* (4 cm), in 1 m, Walindi, Papua New Guinea.

Some of the richest coral growths occur in shallow water on
wave-protected back reefs. Coral diversity declines rapidly with
increased depth; most reef-building species occur in less than 20 metres.

Lizard Island, Great Barrier Reef, Australia.

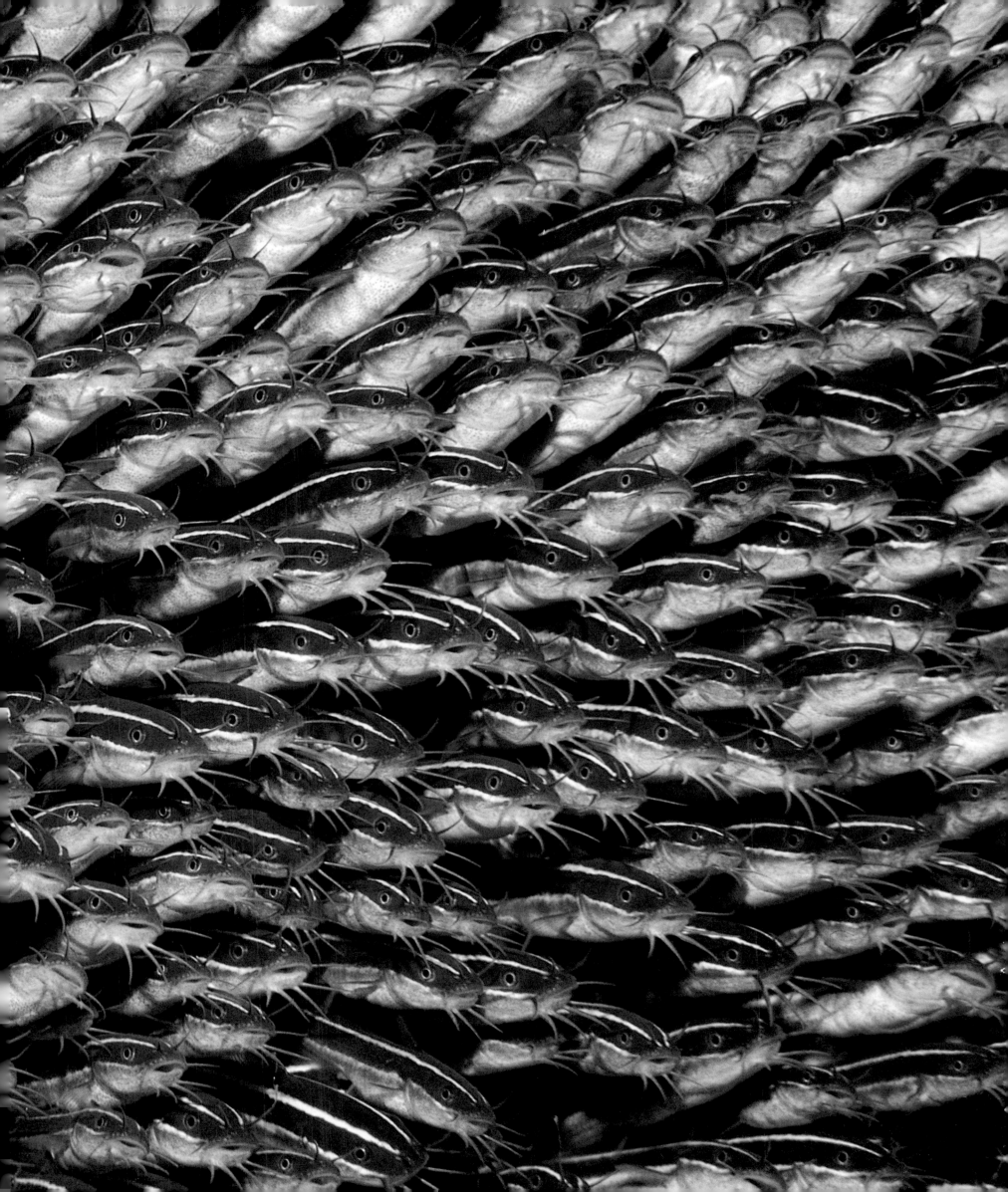

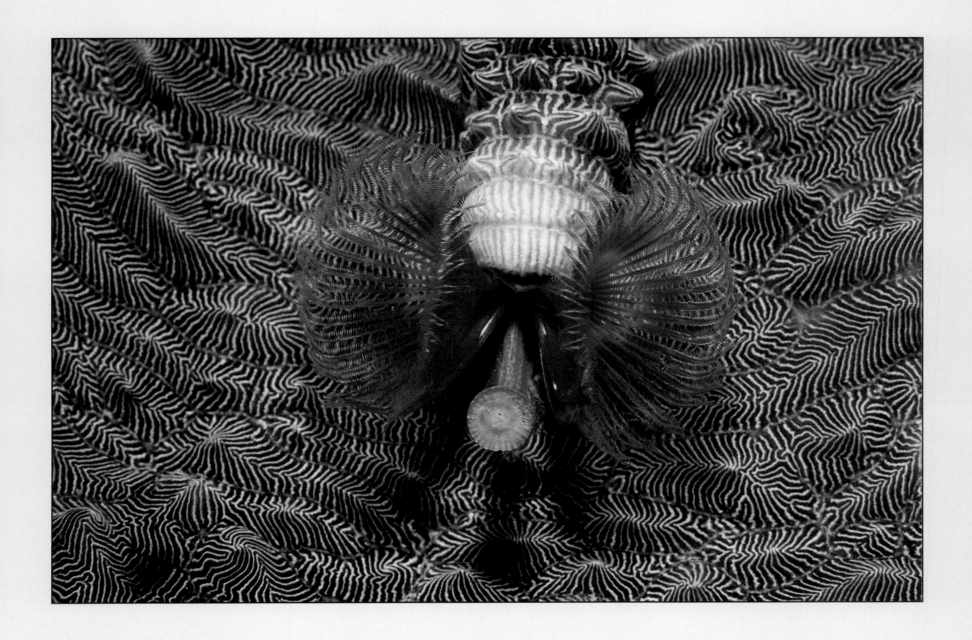

Postlarval worms colonize the surface of hard corals and secrete a tube,
killing the surrounding polyps. New coral rapidly surrounds the tube.
The worm produces additional tube material to keep pace with the growing coral.

Coral Tube Worm, serpulid, (2.5 cm), in 12 m, Maumere, Flores, Indonesia.

Previous page: Juvenile catfishes band together in tight formations,
with individuals actually in contact with one another. The aggregation takes on
the appearance of a much larger animal, reducing the chances of predation.

Striped Catfish, *Plotosus lineatus* (5 cm), in 12 m, Manado, Sulawesi, Indonesia.

Numerous micro-habitats occur on a typical coral reef, even a small section
as seen here. Each fulfils specific requirements for a particular community of
organisms, including the visible fishes and a multitude of unseen inhabitants.

Jackson Reef, Gulf of Aqaba, Red Sea, Egypt.

This unusual crab lives on the surface of giant barrel sponges.
The body is covered with numerous hairs that disguise its shape
and also sense movement in the surrounding environment.

Fairy Crab, *Lauriea siagiani* (1.5 cm), in 8 m, Komodo Islands, Indonesia.

Opposite: Coral reef building involves a dynamic process in which the
skeletal remains and other hard parts of marine animals are recycled. These
sediments often consolidate into beachrock, providing a foundation for new growth.

Beach sediment, Lizard Island, Great Barrier Reef, Australia.

The Royal Urchin picks up bits of debris to cover itself, probably to hide from
echinoderm-feeding fishes. Leaves, small shells, and coral rock are normally used,
but in this case it is also decorated with a *Dendronephthya* soft coral.

Mespilia globulus (8 cm), in 20 m, Komodo Islands, Indonesia.

Opposite: The Komodo Islands are famous for their spectacular encrusting marine life.
Every square metre is carpeted by diverse and colourful invertebrate communities.

Encrusting organisms, unidentified, in 10 m, Komodo Islands, Indonesia.

A unique combination of colours distinguishes Helfrich's Flame Goby from its
two close relatives. This small fish has the habit of flicking the dorsal and
pelvic fins back and forth, possibly to communicate with other individuals.

Nemateleotris helfrichi (4 cm), in 40 m, Palau.

Opposite: A microscopic view of the tentacle system of a siphonophore.
The tentacles contain components known as zooids, which perform several
specialized functions. These include stinging, feeding, and reproduction.

Unidentified siphonophore, Lizard Island, Great Barrier Reef, Australia.

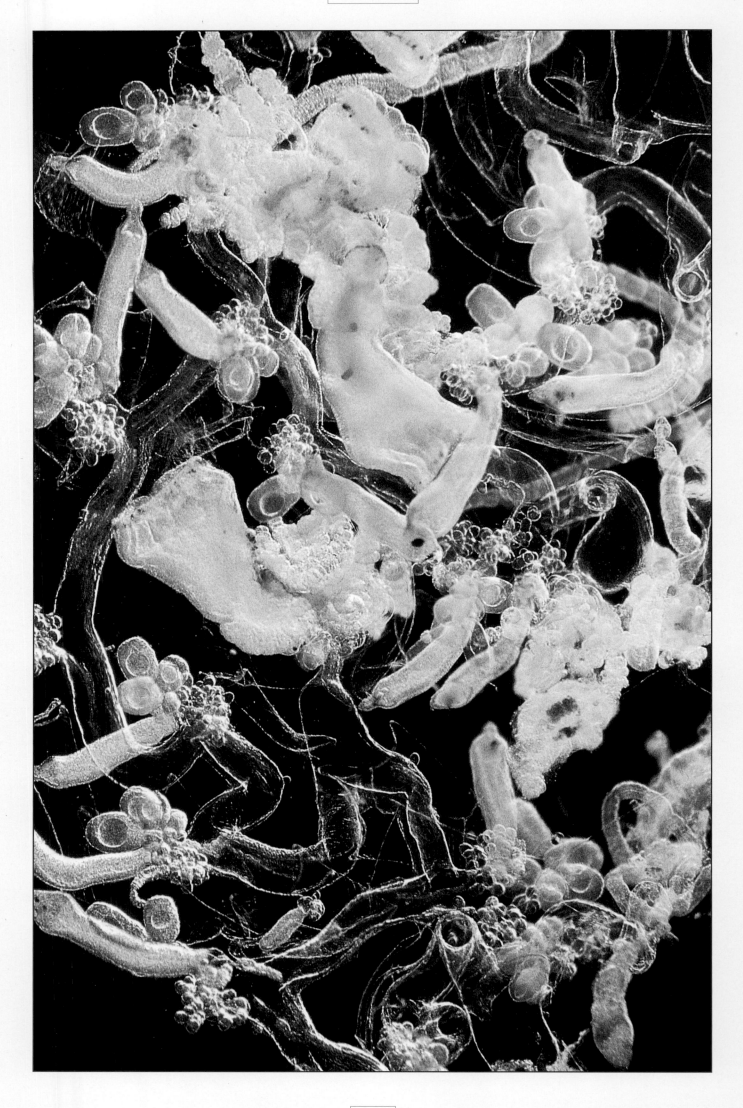

Unusual low tides reveal the intricate architecture of reef-building corals.
Copious secretions of mucous protect the delicate corals from
the sun's damaging rays, but if heavy rainfall occurs the corals may perish.

Flynn Reef, Cairns, Australia.

Opposite: Soft corals are composed of colonies of individual polyps,
which alternately expand and retract. Non-feeding colonies have a smooth,
featureless texture, but erupt into miniature flower gardens when feeding.

Unidentified gorgonian (entire colony 50 cm), in 12 m, Tulamben, Bali, Indonesia.

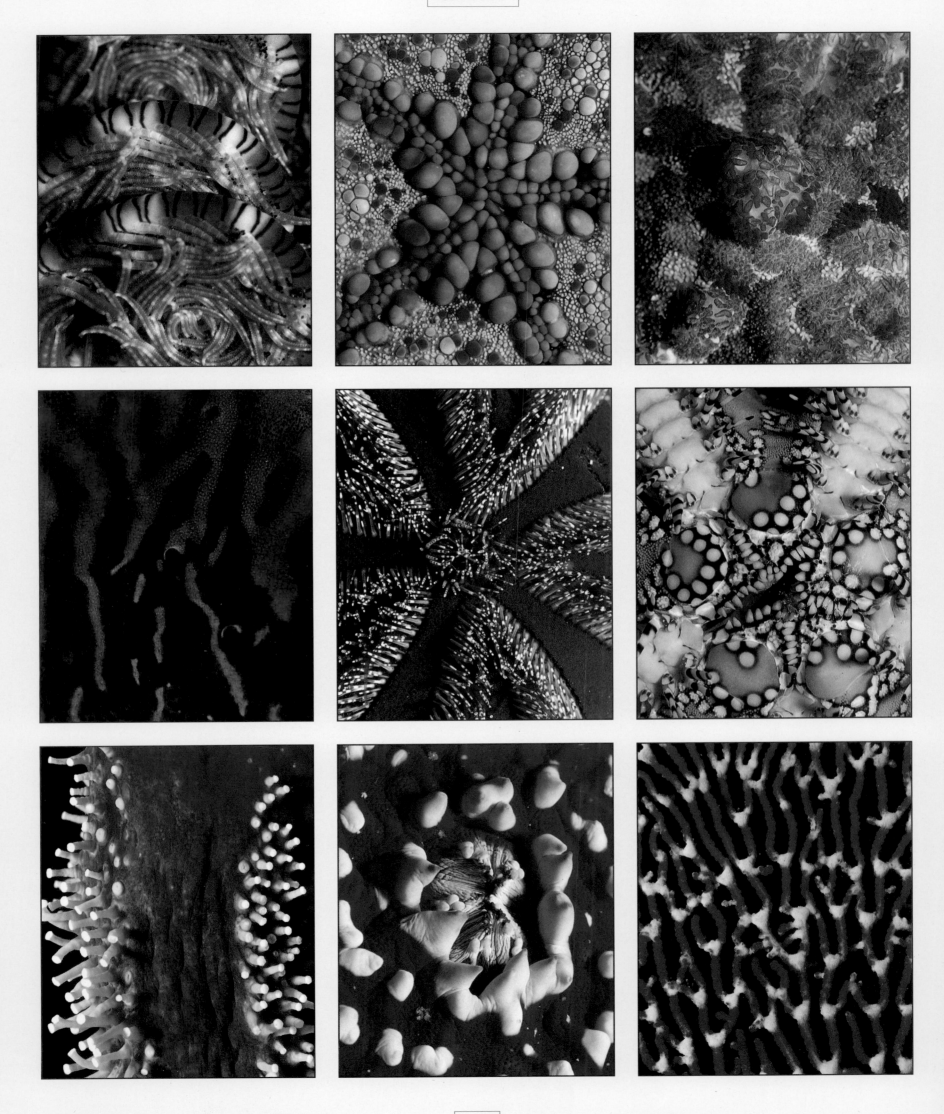

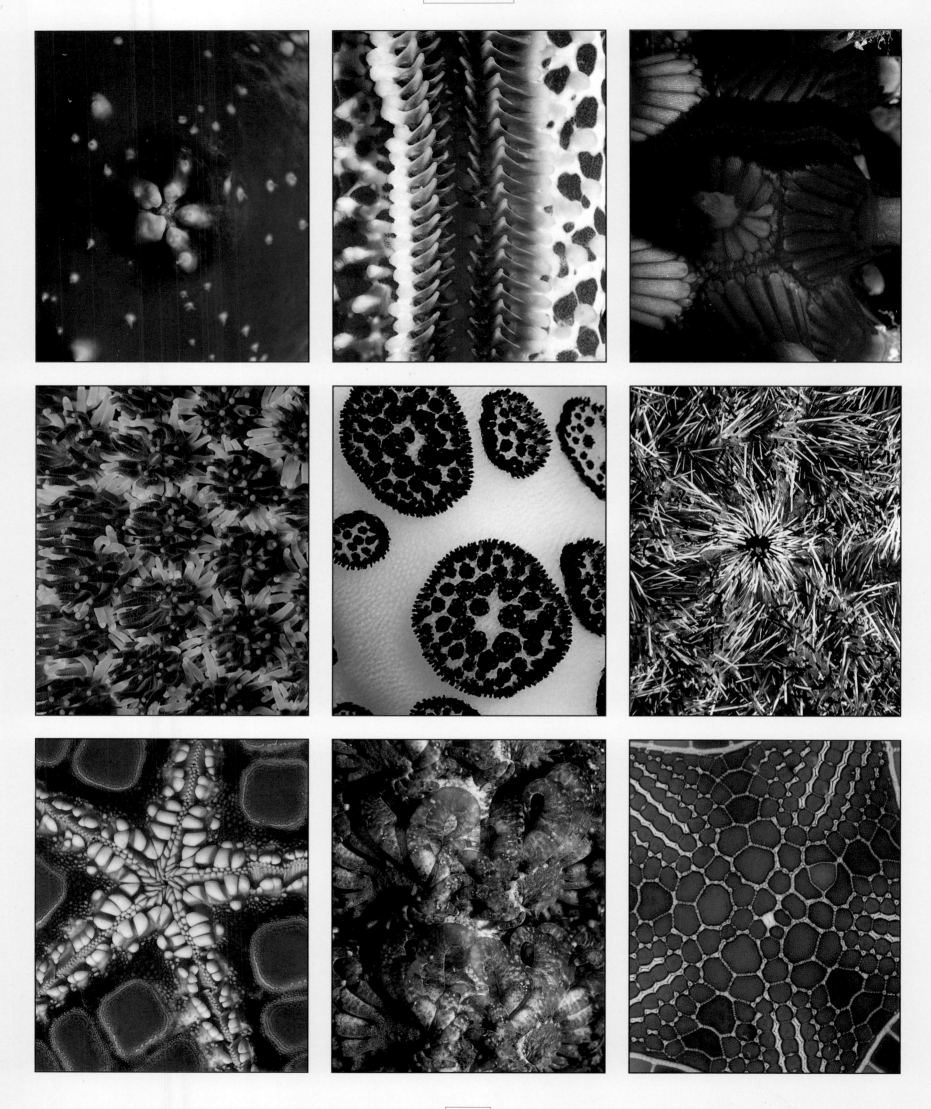

The most delicate forms of hard corals are found in sheltered,
well-protected lagoons. Kranket Lagoon at Madang, Papua New Guinea,
is linked to the sea by a narrow opening, blunting the effect of waves and surge.

Previous pages: A close look at certain marine organisms
reveals intricate designs equalling the finest abstract art. These
patterns are particularly evident in animals showing radial symmetry.

Above left (l to r): Unidentified feather star, Tulamben, Bali, Indonesia; Cushion Star, *Culcita novaeguineae*,
Tulamben, Bali, Indonesia; Unidentified corallimorpharian, Tulamben, Bali, Indonesia.

Centre left: Unidentified sponge, Russell Islands, Solomon Islands; Royal Urchin, *Mespilia globulus*, Pulau Putri,
Indonesia; Green Brittle Star, *Ophiarchna incrassata*, Madang, Papua New Guinea.

Below left: Sea Apple, *Pseudocolochirus violaceus*, Komodo, Indonesia; Starfish, *Euretaster insignius*, Komodo,
Indonesia; Unidentified gorgonian, Komodo, Indonesia.

Above right: Sea Apple, *Pseudocolochirus violaceus*, Komodo, Indonesia; Starfish, *Euretaster insignius*, Komodo,
Indonesia; Slate Pencil Urchin, *Eucidaris metularia*, Komodo, Indonesia.

Centre right: Star Coral, *Galaxea* sp., Madang, Papua New Guinea; Nudibranch, *Jorunna fenebris*, Palau; Sea
urchin, *Tripneustes gratilla*, Gilimanuk, Bali, Indonesia.

Below right: Pentagon Starfish, *Halityle regularis*, Palau; Tubercular nudibranch, *Pteraeolidia ianthina*, Lembeh
Straits, Sulawesi, Indonesia; Longarm Starfish, *Iconaster longimanus*, Bintan Island, Indonesia.

The pattern and shape of the Slender Needle Shrimp closely match its surroundings
among the branches of black corals and sea whips. When danger approaches, it
presses its elongate body close to its host, rendering it nearly invisible.

Tozeuma sp. (6 cm), in 18 m, Tulamben, Bali, Indonesia.

The shell, eyes, and tentacles are fully formed in the larval
veliger stage of this gastropod mollusc. The protruding velum
is covered with beating cilia and acts as a propulsion unit.

Unidentified larval gastropod mollusc (4 mm), Lizard Island, Great Barrier Reef, Australia.

Opposite: Any vacant space on the reef is quickly colonized by an array of
competing organisms. This dead gorgonian forms a tenement for both encrusting
and mobile creatures – sponges, tunicates, hydroids, and echinoderms.

Blue tunicate, *Ectinascidia* sp.; red tunicate, possibly didemnid; orange sponge, *Haliclona* sp.;

brittle star, *Ophiothrix* sp. (colony 20 cm), in 20 m; Maumere, Flores, Indonesia.

This comb jelly is literally a swimming mouth. When it contacts
other types of comb jellies (lobate ctenophores) the flexible oral cavity
envelopes its prey, which is sometimes several times larger than the predator.

Beroe ovata (7 cm), in 2 m, Lizard Island, Great Barrier Reef, Australia.

Flasher wrasses perform remarkable courtship dances highlighted by dazzling displays.
Male colours are greatly intensified and the fins are fully extended.

Angular flasher, *Paracheilinus angulatus* (7 cm), in 7 m, Anilao, Batangas, Philippines.

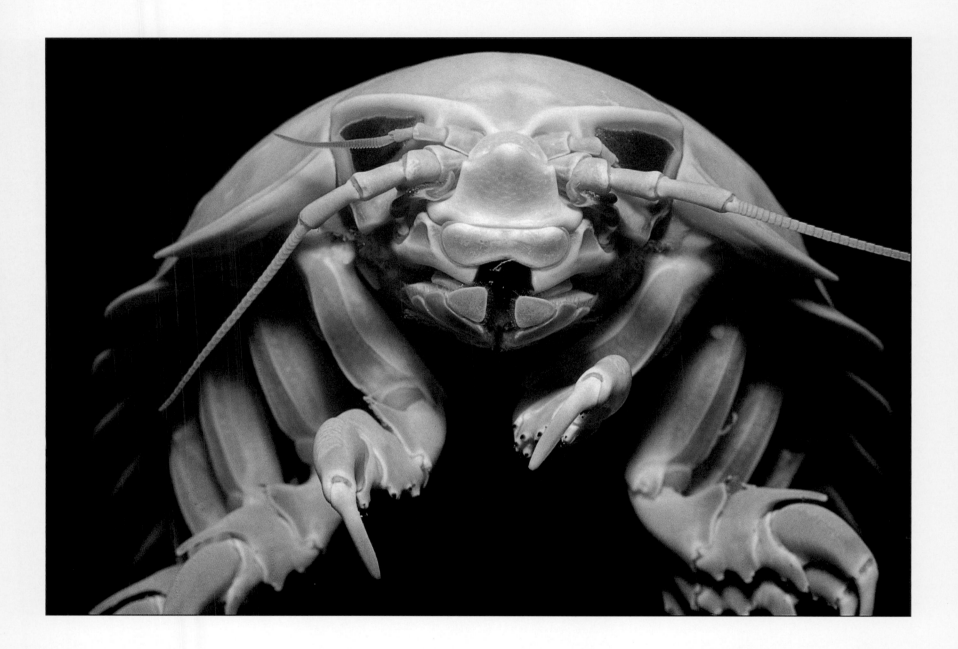

This Darth Vader look-alike is a giant deep-sea isopod, trapped in 1000 metres.
The live specimens were mistakenly placed in a freezer. When retrieved by the
author for photography, they were frozen in a solid block of ice. Miraculously,
they came to life when thawed! They survived due to the similarity of the freezer
conditions and the ambient temperature of their environment, about 1°C.

Bathynomus sp. (20 cm), from 1000 m, continental shelf off Cairns, Australia.

Harp shells trap crabs and shrimps with their huge foot, smothering them
with sand and mucous. The rear portion of the foot can be shed,
and its movement serves to deceive potential predators.

Harpa major (30 cm), in 8 m, Ambon, Indonesia.

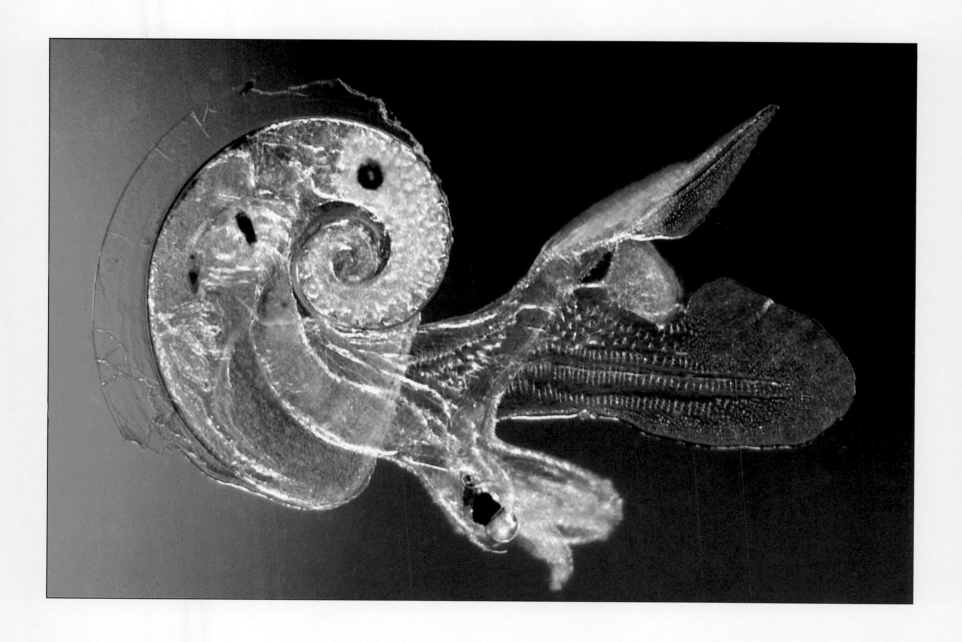

This heteropod mollusc larva swims upside down using the backward-projecting flap as
a sculling fin. The dagger-like operculum angled above has a drogue parachute
apparatus to slow the animal's descent when it stops swimming.

Larval mollusc, *Atlanta* sp. (3 mm), Lizard Island, Great Barrier Reef, Australia.

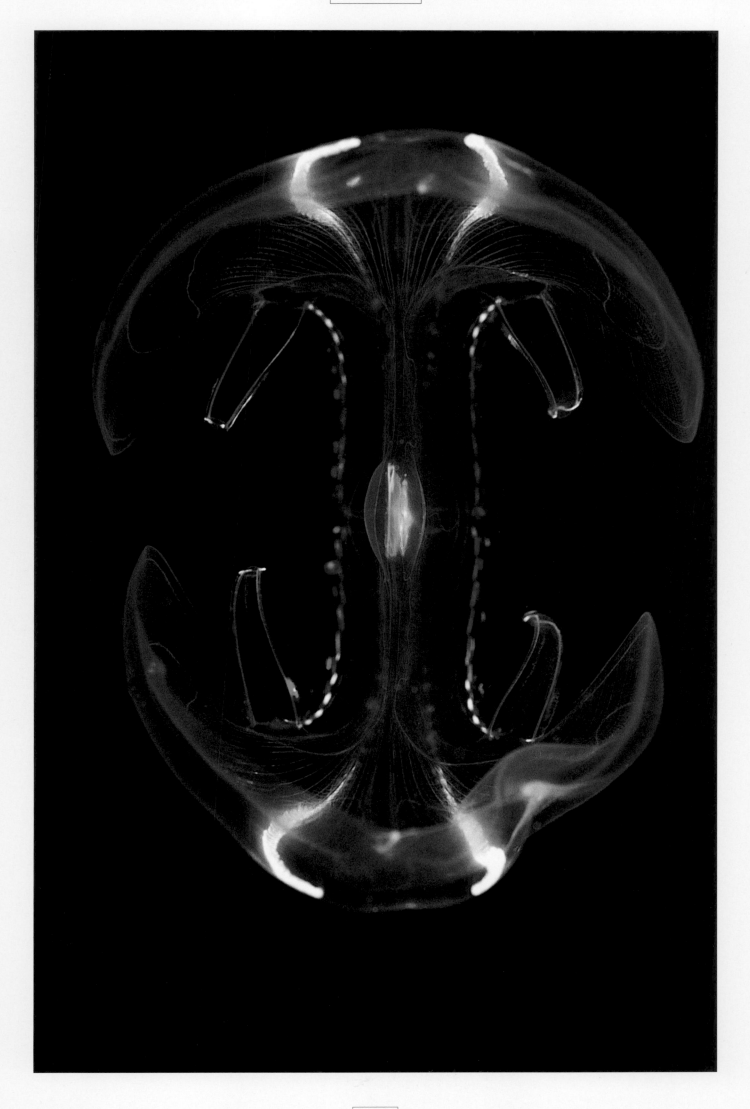

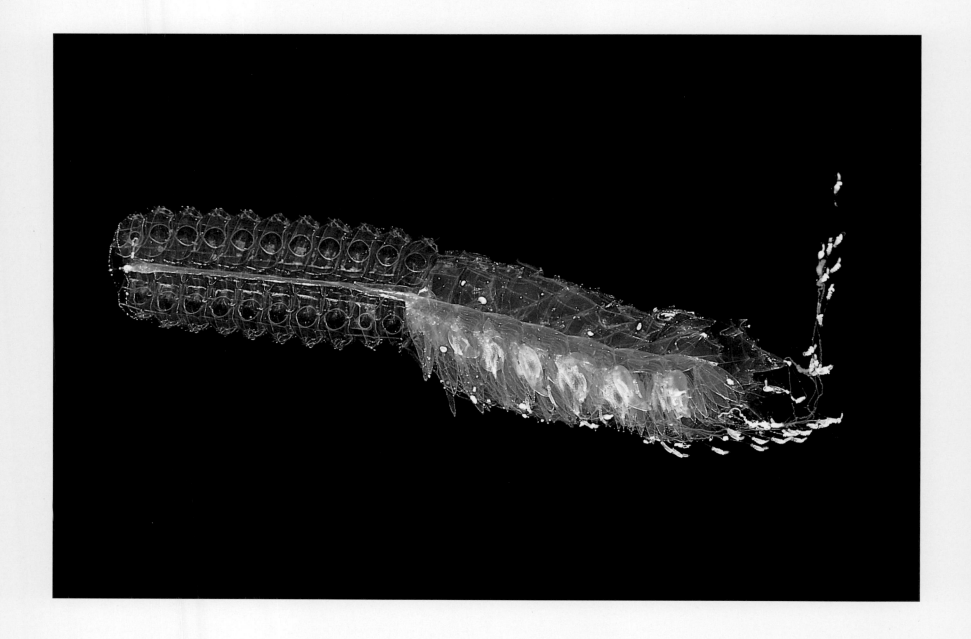

Like an intergalactic explorer this siphonophore is jet-propelled.
It moves by pumping water through its hollow body cavity.
Flotation is aided by a small gas bladder called a pneumatophore.

Nanomia sp. (15 cm), in 5 m, Lizard Island, Great Barrier Reef, Australia.

Opposite: This planktonic butterfly soars high above a coral reef.
The Winged Comb Jelly swims with an exaggerated flapping motion. The
bright colours are produced by fine appendages that reflect light and colour.

Ocyropsis crystallina (5 cm), in 2 m, Lizard Island, Great Barrier Reef, Australia.

Copulating swimmer crabs form a mirror image on an Indonesian sand flat. The larger
male walks or runs unhindered, in spite of the female clinging tightly to his abdomen.

Charybdis sp. (30 cm), in 8 m, Ambon, Indonesia.

The long hairy legs of this early phyllosoma larval stage of a slipper lobster are adapted for clinging onto jellyfishes. This unusual hitch-hiking behaviour is a useful means of dispersal, although the larvae may also swim independently.

Unidentified larval slipper lobster (5 mm), Lizard Island, Great Barrier Reef, Australia.

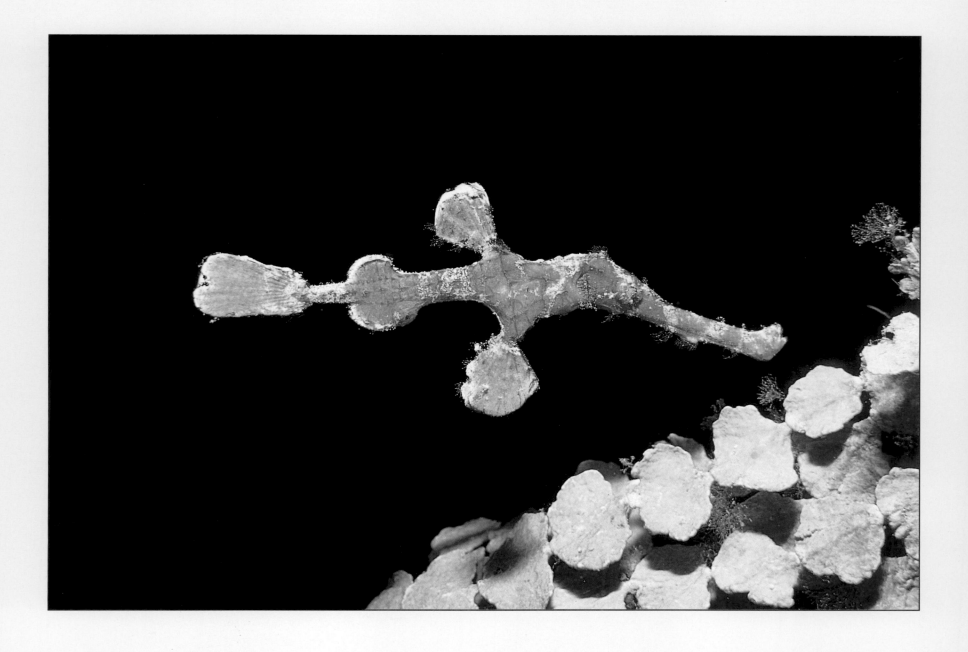

Above, opposite and previous pages: Ghost pipefishes are
seldom seen due to their remarkable camouflage. They assume
an amazing variety of shapes and colours, effectively blending with a
diverse range of organisms, including crinoids, soft corals, and seagrasses.

Previous left: Ornate Ghost Pipefish, *Solenostomus paradoxus* (10 cm), in 12 m,

Lembeh Straits, Sulawesi, Indonesia.

Previous right: Smooth Ghost Pipefish, *Solenostomus* sp. (5 cm), in 12 m, Lembeh Straits, Sulawesi, Indonesia.

Opposite: Halimeda Ghost Pipefish, *Solenostomus* sp. (5 cm), in 12 m, Madang, Papua New Guinea.

Above: Hairy Ghost Pipefish, *Solenostomus* sp. (10 cm), in 6 m, Lembeh Straits, Sulawesi, Indonesia.

A lack of rainfall and its consequent run-off, combined with
sheltered conditions, provide the ingredients for pristine clarity on
Red Sea reefs. Underwater visibility may surpass 40 metres in some places.

Gordon Reef, Gulf of Aqaba, Red Sea, Egypt.

Opposite: Although sand habitats are notoriously poor for shelter,
they harbour a surprising number of predators. Buried eels
can explode from beneath the sand, seizing unsuspecting victims.

Above: Crocodile Eel, *Brachysomophis crocodilinus* (80 cm), in 10 m, Christmas Island, Indian Ocean.

Below: Scarlet Snake Eel. *Brachsomophis henshawi* (80 cm), in 6 m, Anilao, Philippines.

Deep water is exciting but vastly overrated. Shallow, sunlit waters offer
far more opportunities to examine the reef in detail. Many of the
photographs in this book were taken shallow, some in less than 1 metre.

Jackson Reef, Gulf of Aqaba, Red Sea, Egypt.

Opposite: The Blue Jawfish darts suddenly upwards after switching on
bright luminous colours during courtship displays. Luck and patience
are required to photograph the action before it retreats to the burrow.

Opistognathus variabilis (7 cm), in 8 m, Lembeh Straits, Sulawesi, Indonesia.

Porcelain crabs are common in a variety of reef habitats, but are seldom seen due to
their shy and retiring habits. This previously undetected species, which is new to
science, was found hidden among the outer ridges of a large Barrel Sponge.

Blue Porcelain Crab, *Porcellana* sp. (1.5 cm); Barrel Sponge, *Xestospongia testudinaria*, in 14 m, Tulamben, Bali,
Indonesia.

The Ringwrasse undergoes distinct colour changes during its life cycle, which involves
sex change. Horizontally striped juveniles transform to vertically barred males or
females. The most intense colours occur in terminal adult males, as shown.

Hologymnosus doliatus (35 cm), in 2 m, Tulamben, Bali, Indonesia.

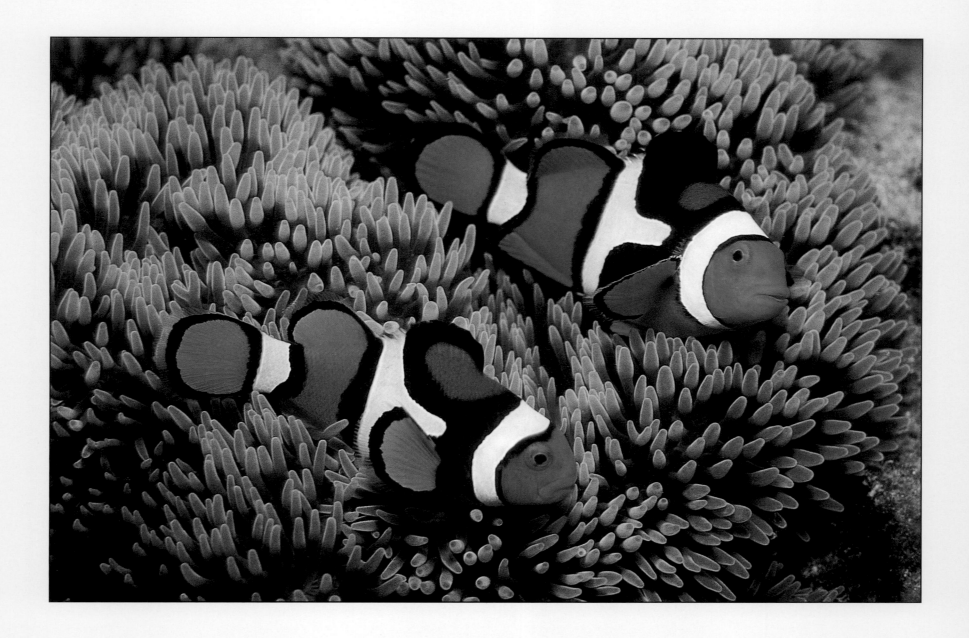

Anemonefishes always form permanent pairs. Breeding occurs monthly
for most of the year. The eggs are laid at the base of the anemone
and guarded by the parents for about one week until hatching.

Above: Clown Anemonefish, *Amphiprion percula* (5 cm), in 2 m, Madang, Papua New Guinea.

Opposite: Anemonefish eggs, *Amphiprion clarkii* (1.5 mm), in 4 m, Tolandono, Tukang Besi, Indonesia.

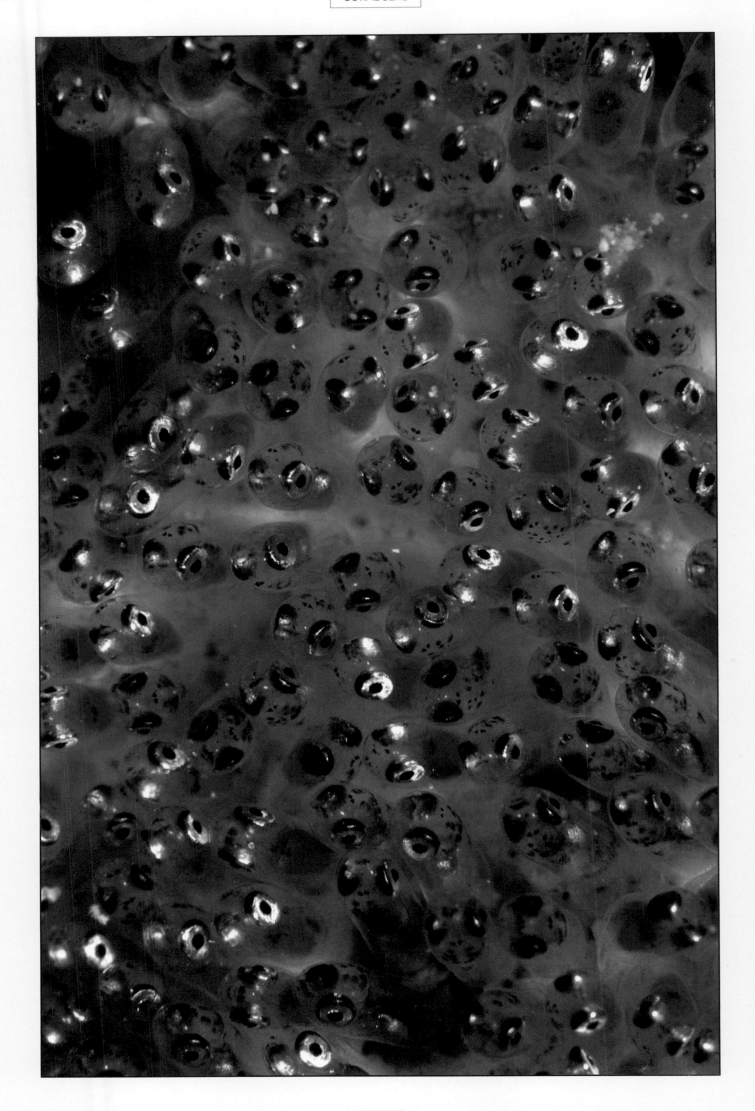

A Giant Moray is mesmerized by the attentions of a pair of cleaner wrasses.
Normally the eel remains well-hidden in crevices, but has visited this
cleaning station to be serviced by these parasite removers.

Gymnothorax javanicus; Cleanerfish, *Labroides dimidiatus* (7 cm), in 10 m,

Jolanda Reef, Sharm-el-Sheikh, Red Sea, Egypt.

Opposite: A magnificent lake occupies most of Kakaban Island,
off the northeastern coast of Kalimantan, Indonesia.
It teems with jellyfishes, by far the most dominant organism.
This unique habitat only occurs here and at Palau in the western Pacific.

Jawfishes are one of the most fascinating groups for behavioural scientists.
They exhibit a wide range of social interactions. Intruders are
summarily ejected if they attempt to share a burrow.

Randall's Jawfish, *Opistognathus* sp. (10 cm), in 4 m, Ambon, Indonesia.

Permanent lifetime bonds are formed by some fishes. This pair of Blueband Gobies
were inseparable, even while foraging well-away from the protection of their burrow.

Valenciennea strigata (15 cm), in 12 m, Tulamben, Bali, Indonesia.

Pearlfish live symbiotically with sea cucumbers. Rarely seen
in the open, they live within the gut cavity of their host, exiting
and re-entering via either the mouth or anus, head or tail first.
Encheliophus homei (15 cm); Leopard Sea Cucumber, *Bohadschia argus* (30 cm), in 10 m,

Madang, Papua New Guinea.

The large and colourful Spanish Dancer nudibranch deposits a flowery corsage of eggs.
The bright red mass probably inherits the inedible qualities of the parents.
It is deposited in exposed locations, but ignored by predators.

Egg mass of Spanish Dancer nudibranch, *Hexabranchus sanguineus* (8 cm), in 3 m, Tulamben, Bali, Indonesia.

Opposite: Brightly margined sea slugs in the family Aglajidae are found on sand
bottoms. After copulation, the female will later envelop herself in a peculiar egg bubble.
Once her work is finished, the transparent egg mass is anchored until hatching.

Above and below: Tailed Sea Slugs, *Chelidonura varians* (4 cm), in 18 m, Tulamben, Bali, Indonesia.

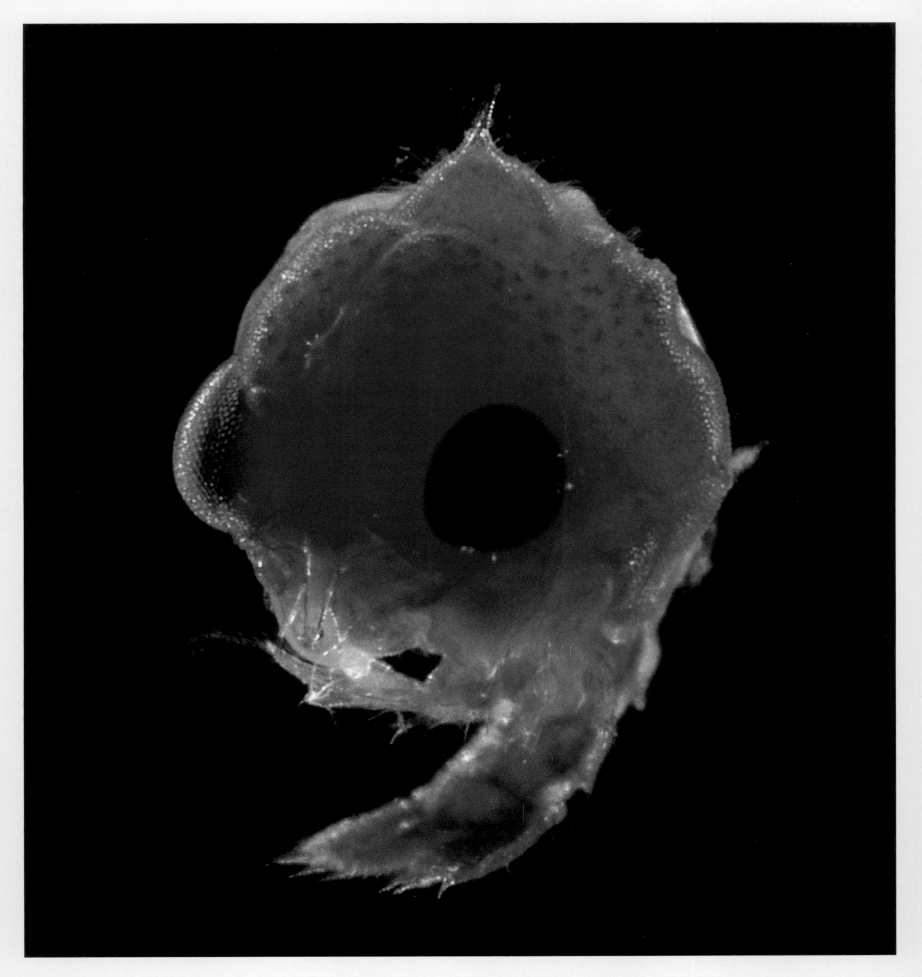

Reef crab larvae pass through a series of distinct growth stages
before metamorphosing into adults. This first-stage zoea
is typified by large compound eyes and a diminutive dorsal spine.

Unidentified larval crab (1.5 mm), Lizard Island, Great Barrier Reef, Australia.

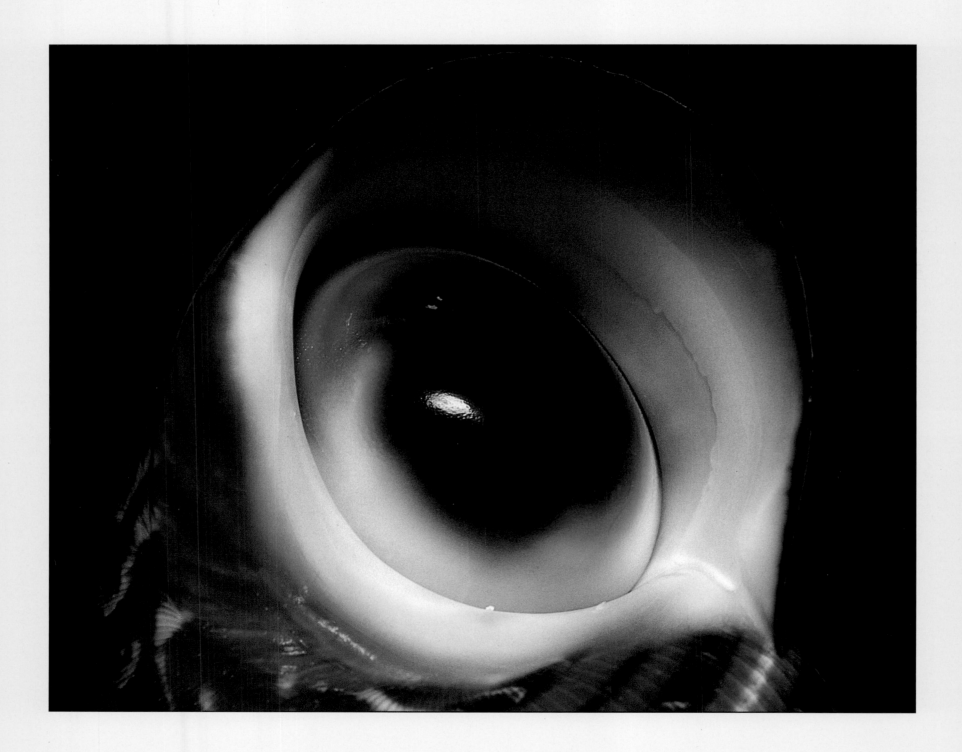

The operculum of this turban shell is aptly referred to as a 'cat's eye'.
This rock-hard structure covers the opening of the shell when
the animal's 'foot' is retracted, protecting its internal organs.

Turbo petholatus (operculum 1 cm), in 5 m, Russell Islands, Solomon Islands.

This miniature hermit crab lives in hard corals and fire corals, rather than
in shells, like its cousins. It filters food by fanning the feathery antennae
through the water and then wiping the trapped plankton into its mouth.

Coral Hermit Crab, *Paguritta* sp. (5 mm), in 3 m, Tulamben, Bali, Indonesia.

The Moon Jellyfish is common in all tropical seas, forming
impressive aggregations during periods of calm weather. Despite the
fringe of numerous tentacles, its mild sting poses no threat to swimmers.

Aurelia aurita (10 cm), in 1 m, Lizard Island, Great Barrier Reef, Australia.

Microscopic view of the first 14 days in the life of a hard coral

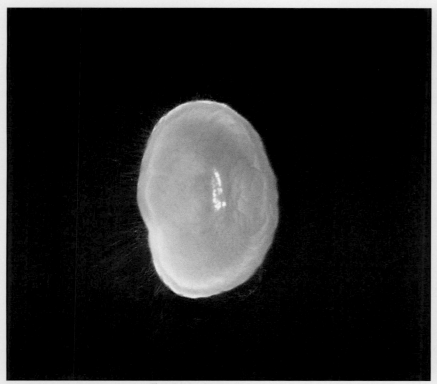

Freshly released planulae

One day after settling

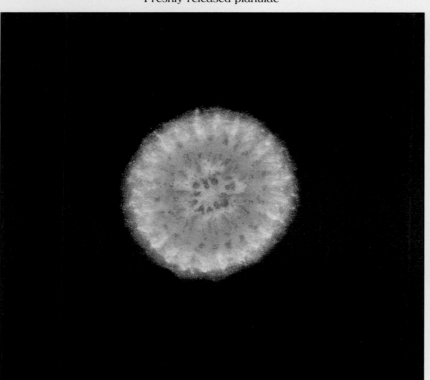

Fourth day

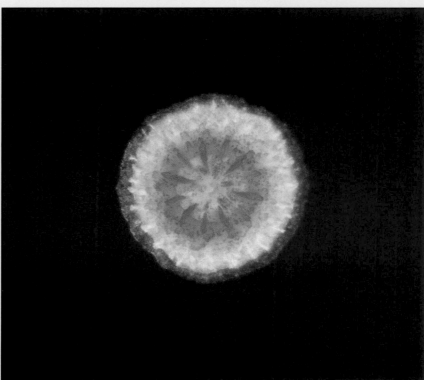

Seventh day

Tenth day

Twelfth day

Fourteenth day, now showing typical coral structure

Mature colony

Seriatopora corals spawn on a lunar cycle. The tiny mobile offspring,
known as planulae, swim by beating microscopic hairs on the margin
of the disc. When a suitable clean substrate is contacted, they
attach permanently and begin to grow into a coral colony.

Coral growth cycle, *Seriatopora hystrix*, Lizard Island, Great Barrier Reef, Australia.

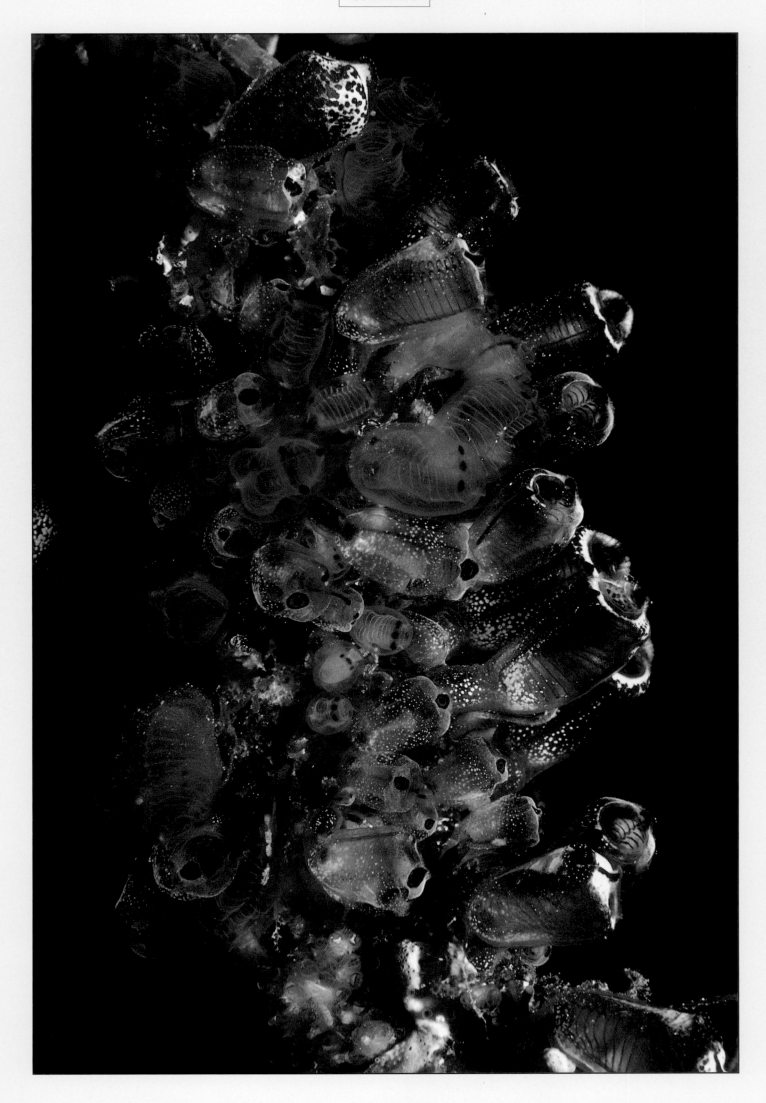

A classic atoll includes a central lagoon surrounded by a chain of
shallow reefs and low islets. This structure results from successive layers
of living coral growing around the fringe of a sinking volcanic island.

Kuop Atoll, Caroline Islands. Photo by Dr Pat Colin.

Opposite: Ascidians attach to a variety of surfaces,
including other tunicates. Mixed colonies containing more than
one species often result when living space is in short supply.

Mixed unidentified ascidians (1 cm), in 15 m, Tolandono, Tukang Besi, Indonesia.

Only a devout diver can fully appreciate this tranquil reef scene.
Dead calm spells, lacking the hindrance of wind and waves,
occur when least expected and never last long.

Surface reflection, Semporna, Borneo, Malaysia.

Opposite: The bright colours of these sea squirts are
derived from a variety of pigments located in the tunic,
blood cells, and the calcareous spicules embedded in the body wall.

Blue Tunicate, *Rhopalaea crassa* (2 cm); other tunicates, didemnids, in 10 m, Tulamben, Bali, Indonesia.

Bare surfaces are instantly colonized by marine organisms. A sunken object can form a handy marker for scientists. It allows them to determine the growth rates of various sedentary animals and the process of ecological succession.

Jolanda Reef, Sharm-el-Sheikh, Red Sea, Egypt.

This structure is actually the reproductive organ of a burrowing sponge.
The peculiar sphere is connected to the hidden sponge by the slender stem,
and when ready to reproduce, drifts away to form a new individual.

Burrowing sponge, *Oceanapia sagittaria* (2.5 cm), in 5 m, Manado, Sulawesi, Indonesia.

The steep volcanic sand slopes off northern Bali harbour a wealth of rare and
unusual marine life. The combination of warm tropical seas and cold upwellings from
deep water encourage colonization of rare organisms such as this strange soft coral.

Unidentified soft coral (100 cm), in 20 m, Tulamben, Bali, Indonesia.

Humpback shrimps belonging to the genus *Saron* are among the reef's
most beautiful creatures. They are secretive dwellers of coral crevices, mainly
seen at night. The distinctly humped abdomen is the basis of their common name.

Saron sp. (6 cm), in 12 m, Madang, Papua New Guinea.

Tunicates are sac-like animals with a pair of openings, one for drawing water and
food into the body, and the other for expelling it along with waste. A continuous current
is generated through the animal by the beating of tiny internal hairs.

Spotted Glass Tunicate, *Clavelina* sp. (10 mm); other tunicates, didemnids (4 mm), in 10 m,

Tulamben, Bali, Indonesia.

In rare situations, there is an almost uninterrupted transition between terrestrial and marine growths. Deep-dwelling soft corals grow profusely in this shallow, tree-shaded environment. These conditions were encountered in the Solomon Islands.

Reef meets rainforest, Gibson Islands.

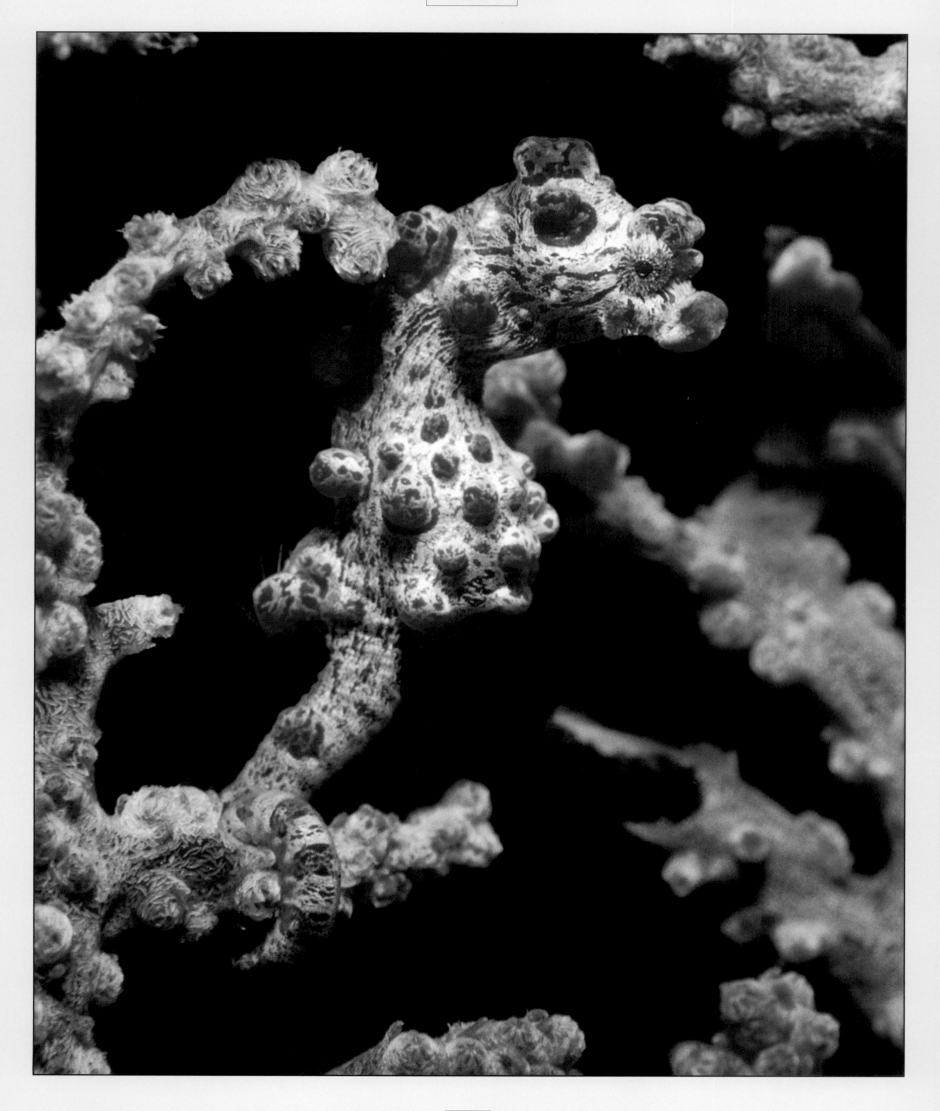

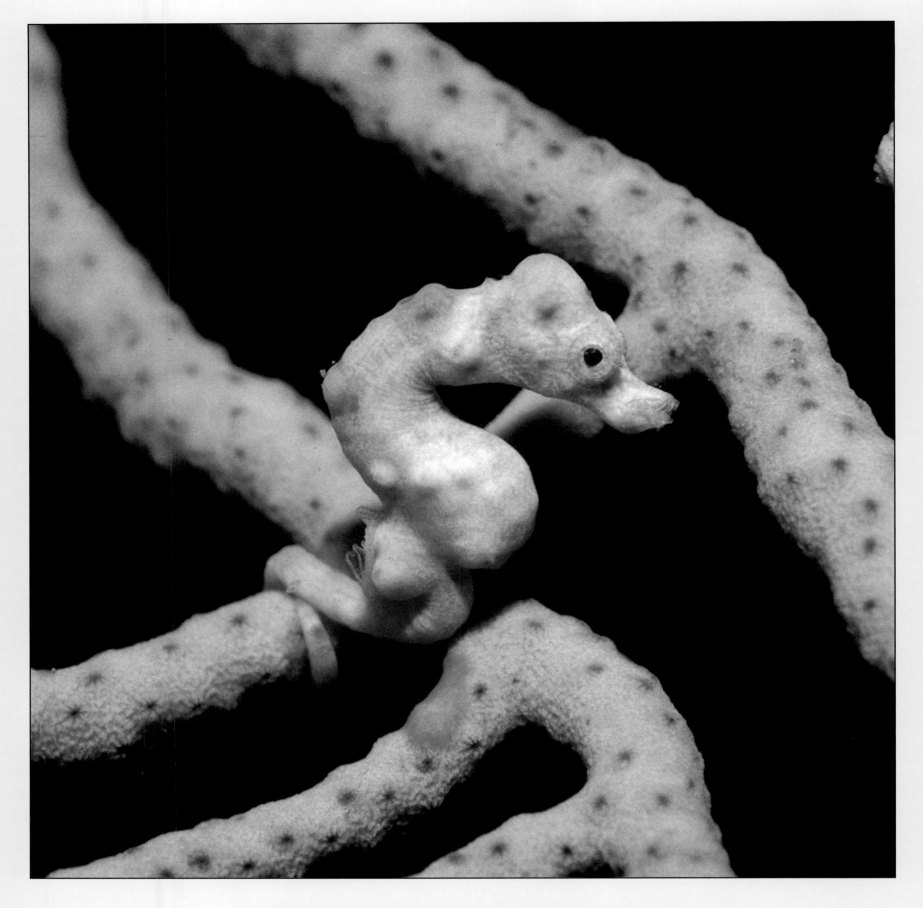

These Pygmy Seahorses are almost impossible to detect.
They live exclusively among the branches of their own special gorgonians.
Their bumpy surface texture perfectly matches the polyp structure of the host seafan.

Above: Pygmy Seahorse, possibly *Hippocampus bargibanti* (1.5 cm); gorgonian, *Subergorgia mollis*, in 20 m,
Lembeh Straits, Sulawesi, Indonesia.

Opposite: Pygmy Seahorse, *Hippocampus bargibanti* (1 cm); gorgonian, *Muricella* sp. in 25 m,
Lembeh Straits, Sulawesi, Indonesia.

An isolated outcrop forms an oasis on a sandy slope at this
Indonesian locality. Strong currents rain a constant barrage of larvae.
Only a lucky few will find precious living space on these tiny reefs.

Miniature reef, in 18 m, Tulamben, Bali, Indonesia.

Opposite: Porcelain crabs are filter feeders. This pair live on a sea pen,
giving them access to planktonic food that passes by in the currents.
When the pen retracts under the sand, it takes its passengers with it.

Pen Crab, *Porcellanella triloba* (1.5 cm); sea pen, *Virgularia* sp., in 12 m, Flores, Indonesia.

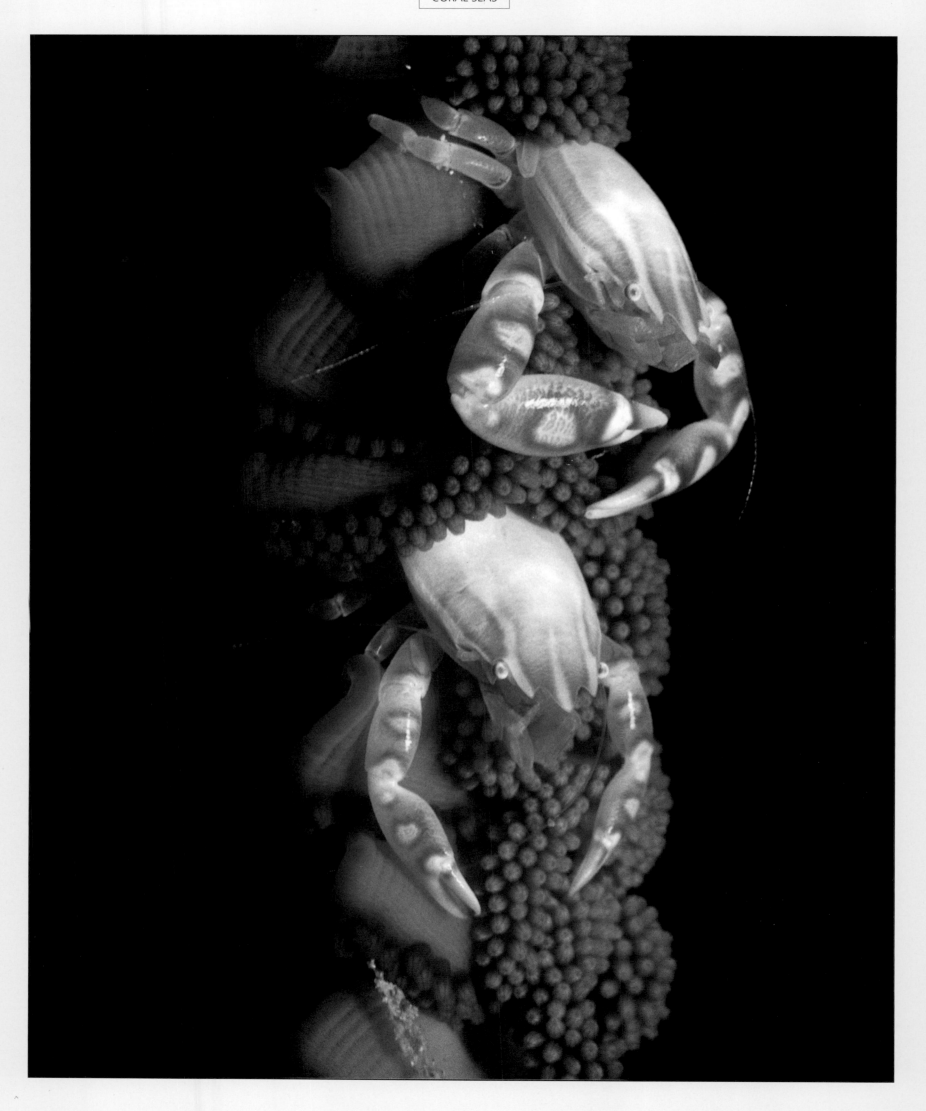

Until recent years the odd Weedy Scorpionfish was virtually unknown to divers.
A spate of sightings in the western Pacific has now made it
a prime target of underwater photographers.

Rhinopias frondosa (12 cm) in 18 m, Ambon, Indonesia.

The reef is populated by myriad seldom-seen animals such as this tiny Flaghead
Triplefin. Although overshadowed by the larger members of the fish community, each
of the numerous types of triplefins has a unique combination of colour and shape.

Ennapterygius sp. (2 cm), Manado, Sulawesi, Indonesia.

This *Periclimenes* shrimp is usually associated with anemones
that periodically retract under the sand. It has forsaken its normal host
in favour of a permanent relationship with this solitary snake eel.

Magnificent Shrimp, *Periclimenes magnificus* (3 cm); Snake Eel, *Ophichthus* sp., in 12 m,

Lembeh Straits, Sulawesi, Indonesia.

The semi-transparent flesh of the tiny Redhead Goby reveals its internal organs.
This fish inhabits rocky reefs in the eastern Pacific Ocean,
frequently in association with sea urchins.

Elacatinus punticulatus (4 cm), in 5 m, Gulf of Chiriqui, Panama.

The bright 'poster coloured' patterns of nudibranchs warn potential predators
of their inedible qualities. The flesh is frequently toxic or distasteful
because of chemical secretions contained within.

Lavender Nudibranch, *Chromodoris* sp. (7 cm), in 12 m, Semporna, Borneo, Malaysia.

Male dragonets often have sail-like dorsal fins, used for attracting mates and
confronting male competitors. This species, like most dragonets, spawns at dusk.

Moyer's Dragonet, *Synchiropus moyeri*. (5 cm), in 9 m, Tulamben, Bali, Indonesia.

Opposite: This solitary anemone normally feeds at night, capturing
small planktonic animals with its long graceful tentacles. When the photographer
illuminated it with a bright light the arms retracted instantaneously.

Possibly *Alicia rhadina* (6 cm), in 3 m, Tulagi, Solomon Islands.

Even the experts are baffled by this peculiar encrusting growth on the stem of a deep water soft coral. Although still undetermined, it is most likely a type of cnidarian.

Unidentified encrusting organism (colony height 8 cm), in 58 m, Tulamben, Bali, Indonesia.

Opposite: This shrimp closely resembles the Elegant Squat Lobster. It was found among the spines of the toxic Ornate Sea Urchin, host to a variety of symbiotic animals, including other shrimps, crabs, and molluscs.

Mimic Shrimp, *Allopontonia iaini* (1 cm); Ornate Sea Urchin, *Asthenosoma varium*, in 20 m, Palau.

It's easy to understand why this centimetre-long transparent shrimp has avoided
detection by scientists until now. It was discovered through the author's lens
while he was photographing the 'ultrastructure' of a Bubble Coral.

Invisible Shrimp, pontoniine (1 cm); Bubble Coral, *Pleurogyra sinuosa*, in 16 m, Manado, Sulawesi, Indonesia.

Opposite: Tiny porcelain crabs cluster together on the surface of
a spiky soft coral. The crabs are perfectly camouflaged;
even their markings match the spicule matrix of the coral.

Pink Porcelain Crab, *Lissoporcellana* sp. (8 mm); spiky soft coral, *Dendronephthya* sp., in 20 m,
Tulamben, Bali, Indonesia.

Thousands of picturesque islands dot the seas of the Indo-Australian Archipelago,
the vast region extending from the Malay Peninsula to Melanesia.
Many remain uninhabited to this day.

Restorff Island, Walindi, Papua New Guinea.

The Royal Dottyback's striking colouration makes it a favourite of marine aquarists.
It lives in coral crevices on steep slopes, spending much of the time
hidden from view, but making brief forays into the open.

Pseudochromis paccagnellae (6 cm), in 18 m, Tulamben, Bali, Indonesia.

This photograph was intentionally posed to show the vivid colour pattern
on the pectoral fins of this unusual scorpionfish. The Demon Stinger
is actually well-disguised in its normal environment on the bottom.

Inimicus didactylus (12 cm), in 4 m, Lembeh Straits, Sulawesi, Indonesia.

Opposite: Marine reserves afford well-deserved protection for a
variety of animals. The epitome of security is reflected in the nonchalant
behaviour of this young Galapagos Sea Lion. Its nap was briefly
interrupted when it lazily opened an eye to inspect the photographer.

Zalophus californicus galapagenis, Isla Santiago, Galapagos Islands.

159

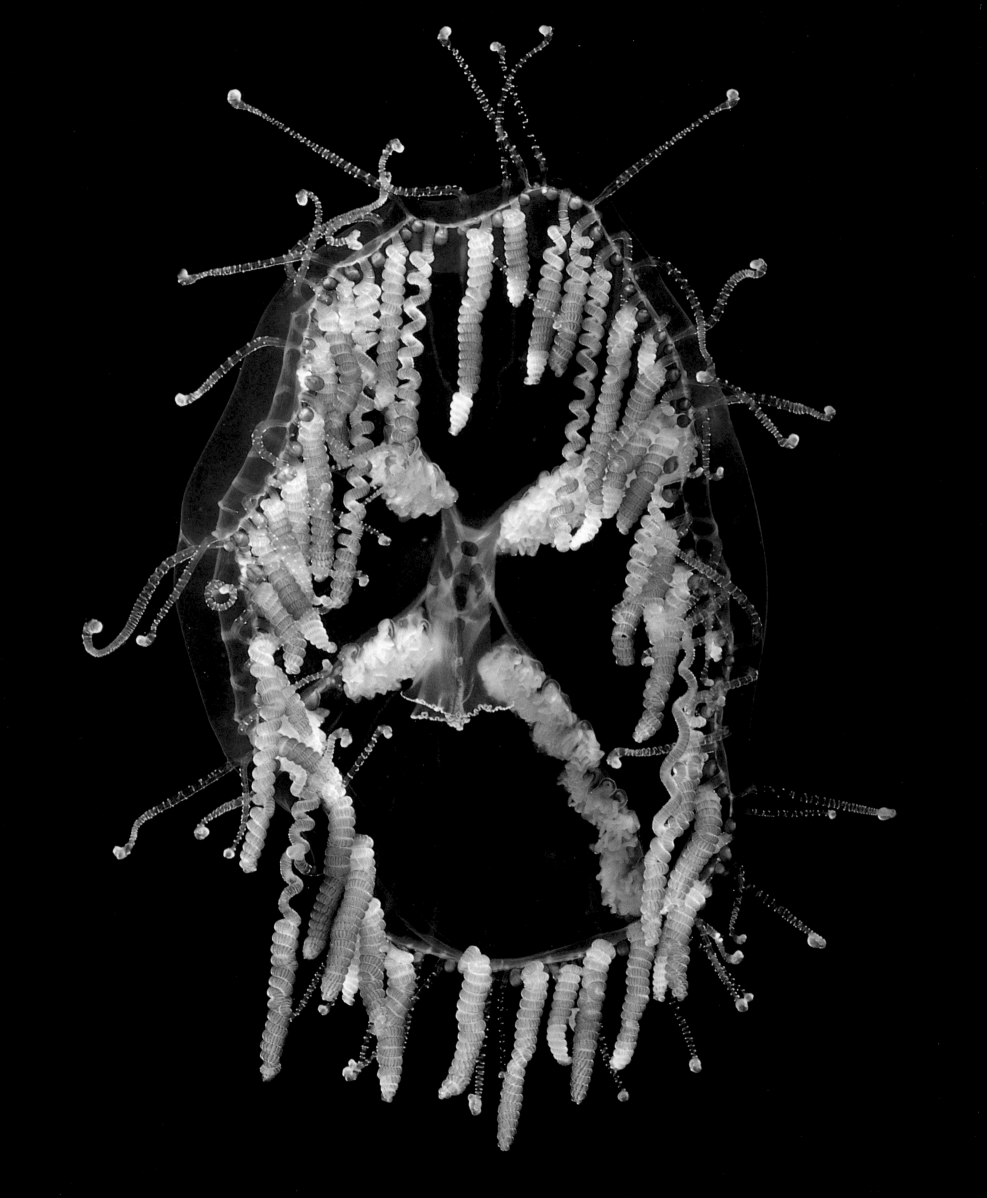

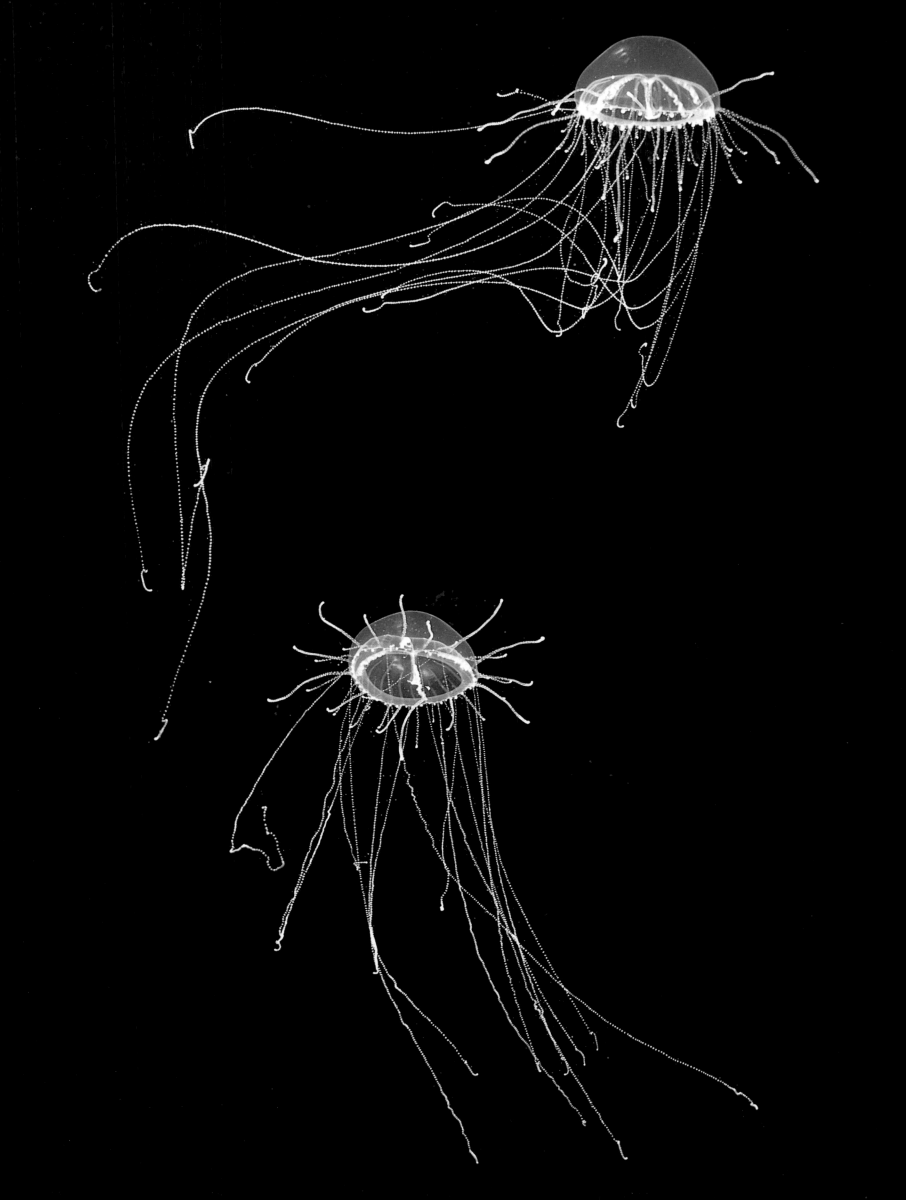

The coral reef is literally a wall of mouths. A wide variety of organisms
filter plankton from the passing currents. These exposed colonial
tube worms differ from most of their relatives, which live in burrows.

Elat Tube Worm, *Filogranella elatensis* (colony 10 cm), in 12 m, Manado, Sulawesi, Indonesia.

Opposite: This brittle star occurs with alcyonarian corals, wrapping the arms
tightly around the branches of its host. In contrast to most of its relatives, which
must hide under rocks for protection, it relies on camouflage colours and a tight grip.

Orange-banded Brittle Star, *Ophiothrix* sp. (15 cm), in 25 m, Kota Kinabalu, Borneo, Malaysia.

Previous pages: The tentacles of the Cigar Jelly are retracted during the day.
At night these appendages are fully extended for feeding.
Their tips are jigged as a form of lure to attract plankton.

Left and right: *Olindias phosphorica* (20 cm), in 1 m, Lizard Island, Great Barrier Reef, Australia.

The scavenging Striped Dog Whelk glides along on its
muscular foot, which secretes friction-reducing mucous. The
prominent siphon is used to detect the scent of potential food.

Nassarius glans (4 cm), in 10 m, Russell Islands, Solomon Islands.

Male dottybacks are exhibitionists. Extended fins are an integral part of their
ritualistic courtship display, an excellent ploy that attracts nearby females.

Flame Dottyback, *Labracinus cyclophthalmus* (15 cm), in 2 m, Tolandono, Tukang Besi, Indonesia.

The colourful basslets of the genus *Pseudanthias* are common on outer
reef slopes throughout the Indo-Pacific region. They are miniature members
of the grouper family, specially adapted for feeding on midwater plankton.

Above: Striped Basslet, *Pseudanthias taeniatus* (8 cm), in 15 m, Sharm-el-Sheikh, Red Sea, Egypt.

Opposite above: Threadfin Basslet, *Pseudanthias huchtii* (8 cm), in 15 m, Murray Island, Solomon Islands.

Opposite below: Luzon Basslet, *Pseudanthias luzonensis* (10 cm), in 23 m, Komodo Islands, Indonesia.

Snapping shrimps derive their name from the loud popping noise they produce,
the shrimp's version of cracking its knuckles. The base of the movable tip
of the large claw is snapped back into the notch on the opposing
fixed claw. This species lives symbiotically with gobiid fishes.

Randall's Snapping Shrimp, *Alpheus randalli* (2 cm), in 23 cm, Tulamben, Bali, Indonesia.

Coral reefs are populated by myriad nudibranchs, including
many that remain unknown to scientists. This spectacular new species
was recently discovered at northern Sulawesi.

Redmargin Nudibranch, *Hypselodoris* sp. (4 cm), in 15 m, Lembeh Straits, Sulawesi, Indonesia.

There is a distinct interaction between terrestrial and marine life along
some tropical shores. Decaying land vegetation is colonized by marine animals;
conversely, dead coral debris is used by beach plants to gain a footing.

Sea and shore, Gibson Islands, Solomon Islands.

Opposite: Spiky soft corals grow best when exposed to strong currents.
One of the best places in the world to witness their full range
of spectacular hues and shapes is the Somosomo Straits in Fiji.

Dendronephthya sp. (100 cm), in 18 m, Taveuni.

The intricate structure of many soft corals can only be appreciated at night.
During the day they appear as featureless lumps, but assume
exquisite shapes and movements when nocturnal feeding commences.

Soft coral, *Minabea* sp. (8 cm) in 15 m, Russell Islands, Solomon Islands.

Opposite: Christmas Tree Worms display a multitude of uniform and
mixed colour combinations. Scientists are still baffled by these unusual variations,
which may represent one highly variable or several distinctive species.

Christmas Tree Worms, *Spirobranchus giganteus* (3 cm), in 2-5 m, Solomon Islands and Indonesia.

The Sea Apple uses its feeding arms to net current-borne zooplankton.
The food is then conveyed, one arm at a time, to the mouth. Colouration
of this animal varies widely depending on locality, but is always brilliant.

Pseudocolochirus violaceus (20 cm), in 18 m, Komodo Island, Indonesia.

The Turret Coral reveals its full splendour at night when
the bright-coloured polyps extend their feeding tentacles.
This organism mostly grows on walls of dark ledges and crevices.

Tubastrea sp. (each polyp 1.5 cm), in 15 m, Russell Islands, Solomon Islands.

Aerial view of the famous Seventy Islands of Palau. Heavy rainfall
and unrelenting seas have reshaped the ancient coral-reef landscape.
These types of islands are unique to Palau and neighbouring Southeast Asia.

Opposite: Soft corals can reproduce sexually or asexually by budding.
The protuberance seen here, which contains a small colony of polyps,
will eventually separate and attach on an adjacent section of reef.

Lobophytum sp. (8 cm), in 6 m, Russell Islands, Solomon Islands.

Toadfishes are characterized by a profusion of fleshy appendages
on the head and body. However, this unusual individual has
far more than normal, giving a grotesque spiky appearance.
Spiky Toadfish, *Halophyrne diemensis* (30 cm), in 10 m, Ashmore Reef, northwestern Australia.

Opposite: Mangroves are nurtured by warm tropical seas.
In most areas they thrive along muddy shorelines,
but in some places they coexist in clean water with reef organisms.
Kakaban Island, Kalimantan, Indonesia.

A pair of Harlequin Shrimp carry a living food supply, their own version
of 'meat on the hoof'. The shrimp have severed the blue starfish arm
with their mouth parts, not the decorative nippers, which are used only for
display. This species also consumes the notorious Crown-of-Thorns starfish.

Harlequin Shrimp, *Hymenocera picta* (2 cm), in 1 m, Palau.

Opposite: In the absence of its usual food source, this extraordinary
white anemone has adapted to a carnivorous diet. It feeds exclusively
on the plentiful jellyfish which inhabit this brackish Indonesian lake.

White Anemone, actiniarian (15 cm); jellyfish, *Cassiopia ornata* (10 cm), in 2 m,

Kakaban Island, Kalimantan, Indonesia.

Triplefins are small, inconspicuous fishes common on coral reefs. The Rhinoceros
Triplefin was formerly known only from New Caledonia, but this photo was recently
taken in Indonesia. Only males exhibit the greatly elongate snout.

Helcogramma rhinoceros (3 cm), in 2 m, Tulamben, Bali, Indonesia.

Members of the genus *Amphiprion* live intimately with
tropical sea anemones. The fish is protected from the host's
stinging cells by special chemicals contained in the body mucous.

Pink Anemonefish, *Amphiprion perideraion* (7 cm); Leathery Sea Anemone,

Heteractis crispa (40 cm), in 10 m, Manado, Sulawesi, Indonesia.

Reef meets rainforest. Lush shoreline vegetation at this Solomon Islands locale
overhangs a narrow fringing reef which drops into a 20-metre deep channel.
Organisms from deep water, such as this gorgonian, thrive under the trees.
Gibson Islands.

Opposite: Neighbour organisms generally tend to compete for available
living space. Some, such as these filter feeders, thrive in close proximity,
and may even overgrow each other without detrimental effect.
Encrusted antipatharian: mixed unidentified ascidians and sponges (field of view, 20 cm), in 20 m,
Tolandono, Tukang Besi, Indonesia.

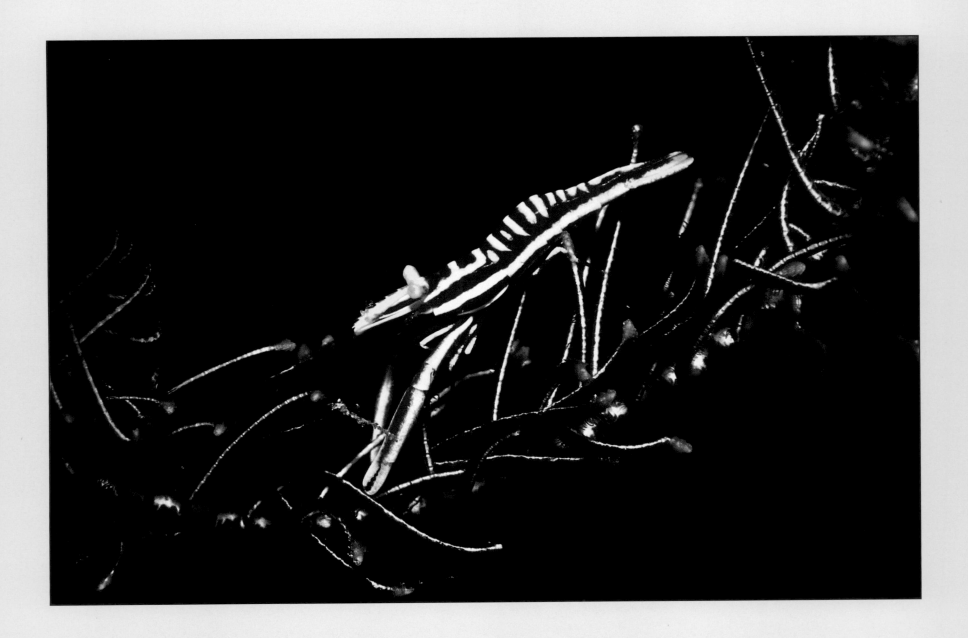

The Feather Star Shrimp probably settles onto its host as a larva, assuming the
colour of its host after several moults. Normally, a lifetime partnership is established,
but if the shrimp needs to find a new feather star, its colour changes to match.

Above: *Periclimenes* sp. (1.5 cm), in 10 m, Tulamben, Bali, Indonesia.

Opposite: *Periclimenes* sp. (1.5 cm), in 12 m, Tulamben, Bali, Indonesia.

Seagrass beds form an integral part of coral reef systems. They are important
nursery areas for a host of organisms, providing shelter and abundant food.
In addition, larger animals, including fishes, turtles, and dugong, feed there.

Kranket Lagoon, Madang, Papua New Guinea.

Opposite: Garden eels live in sandy burrows arranged in colonies that may contain
hundreds or even thousands of individuals. They extend their bodies high above the
burrow entrance while feeding on plankton, but quickly retreat when approached.

Above left: Taylor's Garden Eel, *Heteroconger taylori* (45 cm), in 35 m, Menjangan Island, Bali, Indonesia.

Above right: Flecked Garden Eel, *Heteroconger perissodon* (60 cm), in 2 m, Tulamben, Bali, Indonesia.

Below left: Spotted Garden Eel, *Heteroconger hassi* (60 cm), in 10 m, Tulamben, Bali, Indonesia.

Below right: Banded Garden Eel, *Heteroconger polyzona* (60 cm), in 2 m, Tulamben, Bali, Indonesia.

Flowery external gills are the most remarkable feature of this
striking species of nudibranch. This apparatus allows the animal to 'breathe',
facilitating the exchange of oxygen and carbon dioxide with its aquatic environment.

Flower-gilled Nudibranch, *Gymnodoris aurita* (12 cm), in 10 m, Komodo Islands, Indonesia.

Opposite: These Banded Pipefish disperse over the reef during the day,
but gather in numbers after nightfall. It is uncertain why they assume
this vertical orientation instead of their normal horizontal position.

Doryrhamphus dactyliophorus (12 cm), in 10 m, Ambon, Indonesia.

Shore crabs of the family Grapsidae have evolved a squarish flattened shape,
ideal for squeezing into small rocky crevices. The back pair of legs is not flattened for
swimming, but is modified for climbing and running over rocks, sand, and mud.

Percnon quinotae (15 cm), in 2 m, Tulamben, Bali, Indonesia.

Like an undersea dentist, this Cleaner Shrimp delicately examines the mouth cavity of
a cardinalfish. Small fishes patiently form queues awaiting their turn for this service.

Cleaner Shrimp, *Lysmata amboinensis* (5 cm); Ring-tailed Cardinalfish, *Apogon aureus* (5 cm), in 20 m,

Tulamben, Bali, Indonesia.

The secretive Crinoid Clingfish lives among the arms of feather stars. The symbiotic
relationship is similar to that between anemonefishes and their hosts.
Discotrema echinophila (3 cm), in 10 m, Tulamben, Bali, Indonesia.

Opposite: Calm conditions, warm seas, and a wealth of marine life attract
an ever-increasing number of divers to the Red Sea. This spectacular dropoff
at Ras Muhammed, Egypt, is one of the most popular sites.

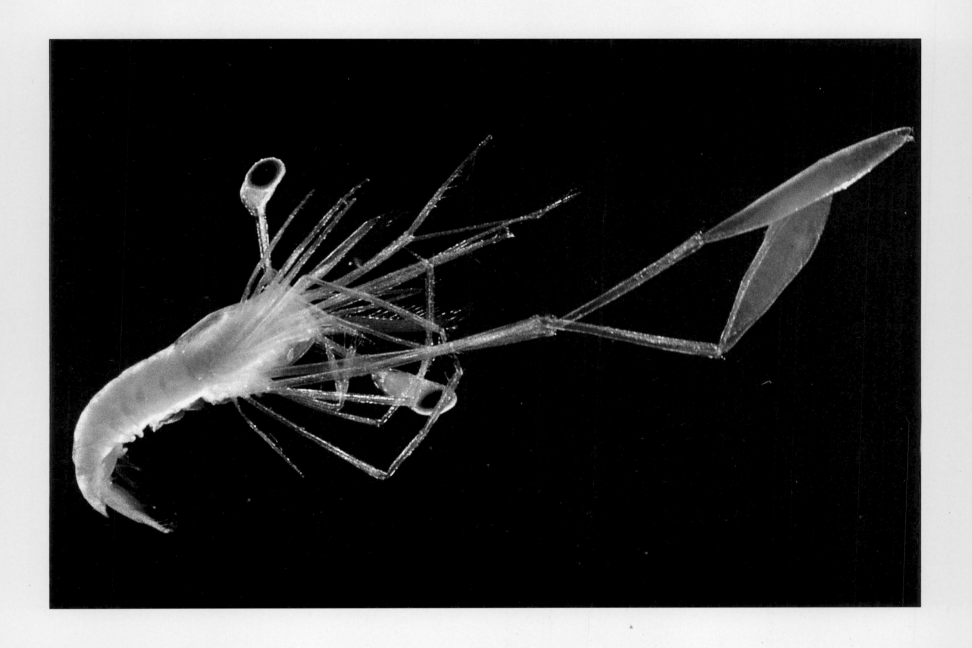

This larval decapod crustacean is found in low numbers among plankton samples.
The long, fragile arms are used as paddles rather than feeding appendages.
Rarely is this delicate animal captured without damage.

Unidentified larval decapod (7 mm), Lizard Island, Great Barrier Reef, Australia.

Sweetlips are nocturnally active. In daytime they shelter close to the reef before
dispersing to feed at dusk. This boldly patterned species is easily approached by divers.

Ribbon Sweetlips, *Plectorhinchus polytaenia* (50 cm), in 25 m, Tulamben, Bali, Indonesia.

This Wentletrap snail lives among and feeds on the living polyps of
Tubastrea corals. Its extended proboscis allows access to
the coral's soft inner tissues. The bright yellow eggs, seen next to the shell,
are sometimes deposited in the remaining cup-like skeletons.

Epitonium billeeanum (12 mm), in 8 m, Tulamben, Bali, Indonesia.

Opposite: Snappers are voracious night predators of fishes and
invertebrates. During daylight hours they often congregate,
seeking cover in shaded locations protected from the current.

Yellow Seaperch, *Lutjanus monostigma* (50 cm), in 12 m, Sharm-el-Sheikh, Red Sea, Egypt.

Young Solomon Islanders take to the water at an early age.
Coral reefs provide valuable sustenance for South Sea islanders.
Most villages are strategically located at water's edge.

Russell Islands.

Opposite: Protected, shady recesses of the reef are carpeted with life.
Here, even though the Thorny Oyster's shell regularly opens and closes,
it provides a base for a variety of organisms.

Spondylus varius (25 cm), in 15 m, Sandfly Passage, Solomon Islands.

Like most of its relatives, this boldly emblazoned cuttlefish alters its colours
like a chameleon. It also has modified tentacles, which work together with fins
that encircle the mantle, allowing it to walk on the bottom.

Flamboyant Cuttlefish, *Metasepia pffeferi* (10 cm), in 6 m, Ambon, Indonesia.

Anglerfishes are nature's ultimate lay-and-wait predators. Their colours
and skin texture blend effectively with the surroundings. Fish prey are lured
within range by a wiggling lifelike bait suspended from the first dorsal-fin spine.

Hairy Anglerfish, *Antennarius striatus* (12 cm), in 10 m, Lembeh Straits, Sulawesi, Indonesia.

The lovely Crosshatch Triggerfish swarms on outer reefs at scattered locations
across the Pacific. It swims high above the bottom while feeding on plankton.

Xanthichthys mento (22 cm), in 15 m, Clipperton Island, eastern Pacific.

Occurring only in tropical seas, the angelfish family has more than 80 distinct species.
They are among the most elegant of the reef's inhabitants.
Members of the genus *Pomacanthus* typify their grace and beauty.

Yellow-faced Angelfish, *Pomacanthus xanthometopon* (35 cm), in 10 m, Walindi, Papua New Guinea.

Opposite: The fertilized eggs of sea cucumbers develop into
planktonic auricularia larvae. They are characterized by bands of cilia
(microscopic projections), used for locomotion and feeding.

Unidentifed larval holothurian (1.5 mm), Lizard Island, Great Barrier Reef, Australia.

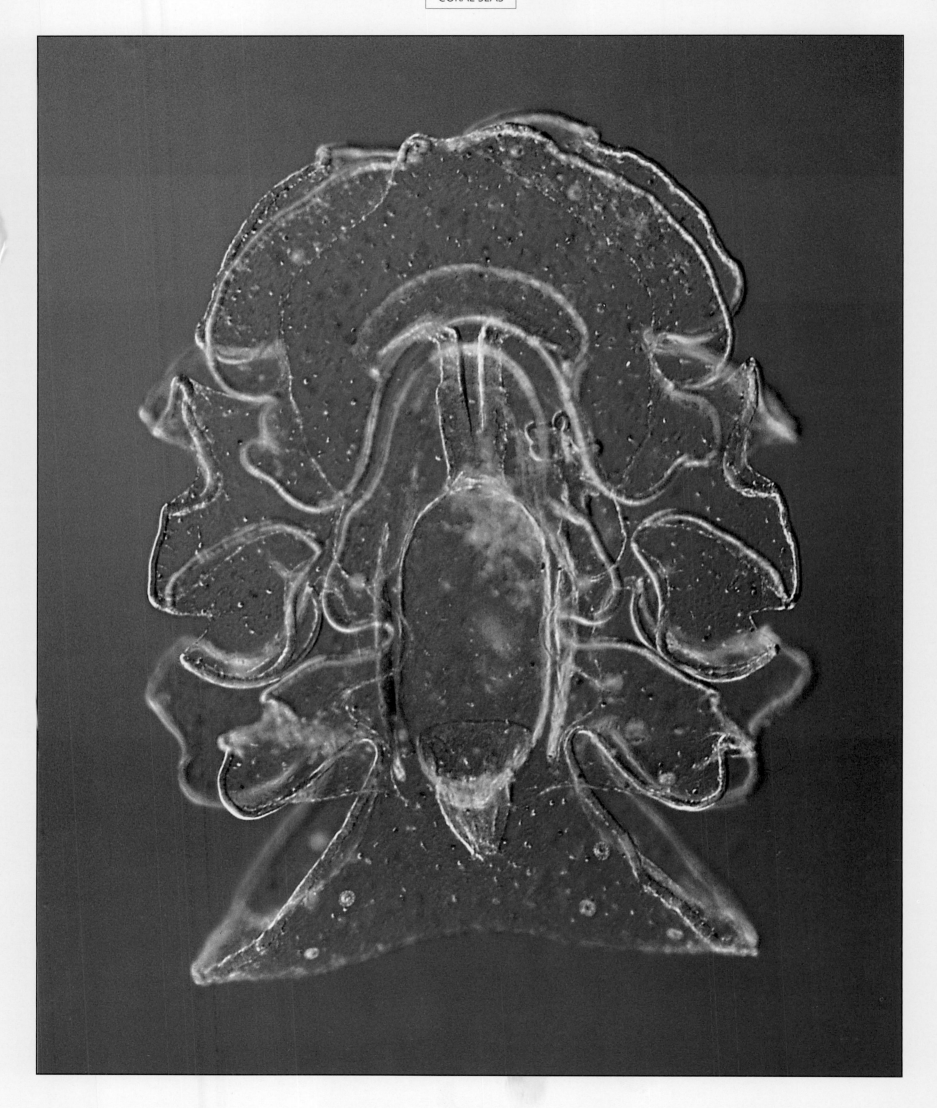

This unusual relative of the rock lobsters is seldom seen,
despite its broad Indo-Pacific distribution. Its small size and
crevice-dwelling habits are responsible for its anonymity.

Orange Lobster, *Palinurella wieneckii* (5 cm), in 12 m, Madang, Papua New Guinea.

Opposite: The larval form of marine animals is sometimes deceiving.
After drifting for weeks at the mercy of winds, waves, and currents,
the transparent young of this cnidarian will eventually settle on
a sandy bottom and transform into a burrowing sea anemone.

Unidentified larval sea anemone (1.5 mm), Lizard Island, Great Barrier Reef, Australia.

A special group of tiny gastropods, sometimes referred to as spindle or
allied cowries, live symbiotically on a wide range of hosts including
black corals, sea whips, gorgonians, and various other soft corals.

Tiger Spindle Cowry, *Crenavolva tigris* (8 mm); unidentified gorgonian, in 20 m, Tulamben, Bali, Indonesia.

Opposite: The elongate snouts of butterflyfishes are adapted for probing hard-to-reach
crevices for invertebrate food. They occur in all tropical reef areas of the world.

Above: Scythe Butterflyfish, *Chaetodon falcifer* (12 cm), in 20 m, Isla Fernandina, Galapagos Islands.

Below: Big Longnose Butterflyfish, *Forcipiger longirostris* (12 cm), in 10 m, Madang, Papua New Guinea.

Polychaete worms have a variety of shapes and lifestyles.
Some are active, mobile animals that crawl over the bottom.
Others are sedentary and unrecognizable as worms.

Unidentified polychaete worm, hesionid, (5 cm), in 18 m, Madang, Papua New Guinea.

Previous pages: Cephalopods have the largest brains and most complex behaviour
of any invertebrate animals. This octopus cleverly carries with it a discarded coconut
and half of a bivalve shell for shelter during excursions over open terrain.

Margined Octopus, *Octopus marginatus* (25 cm), in 5 m, Lembeh Straits , Sulawesi, Indonesia.

A fringing reef hugs the shores of a picturesque bay on Bali's north coast.
Despite periodic volcanic eruptions of massive Mount Agung,
the resilient corals continue to regrow and flourish.

Amed, Bali, Indonesia.

Some species of sea cucumbers spurt sticky threads as a form of protection. These
threads may also contain a toxic substance to enhance their defensive capabilities.

Leopard Sea Cucumber, *Bohadschia argus* (30 cm) in 5 m, Manado, Sulawesi, Indonesia.

Hingebeak shrimps are readily recognized by their long movable rostrum,
hinging from the front of the carapace. This serrated structure is
clearly apparent in the photograph by the yellow colouration.

Galapagos Hingebeak Shrimp, *Rhynchocinetes* sp. (4 cm), in 3 m, Isla Fernandina, Galapagos Islands.

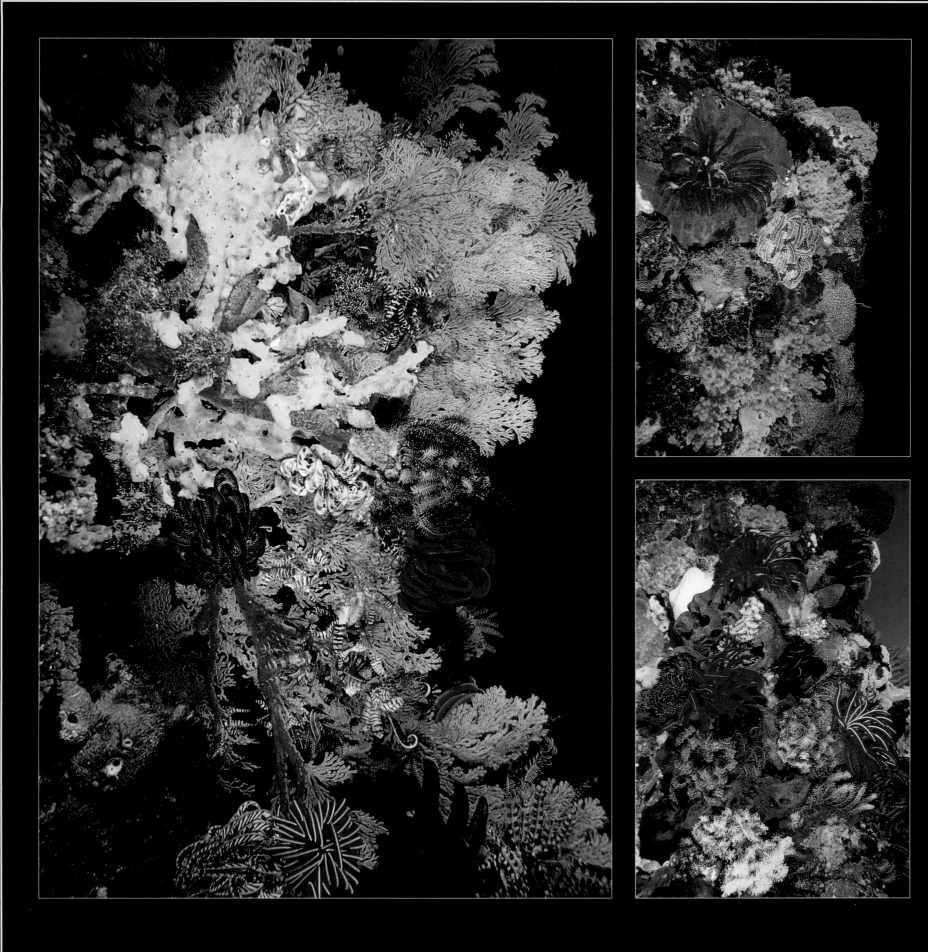

Feather starfish, sponges, and other invertebrates combine in
a riot of colour beneath the waves at this locality. These rich communities
are nourished by cold upwellings, despite their equatorial position.

Mixed invertebrates, unidentified, in 5-15 m, Komodo Islands, Indonesia.

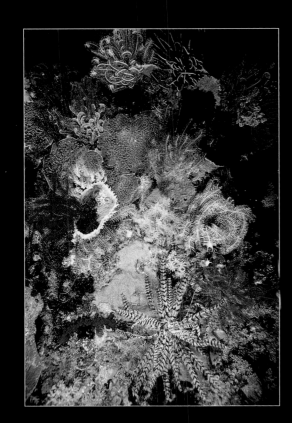

Galatheid crabs resemble miniature lobsters with their long claws and
elongate abdomen, which in this case is curled under the body. They inhabit
a variety of reef environments, from tide pools down to at least 150 metres, usually
on rock or coral substrates. These animals are also known as squat lobsters.

Red Squat Lobster, *Munida* sp. (4 cm), in 18 m, Padang Bai, Bali, Indonesia.

The boldly patterned Arabian Tang inhabits shallow coral reefs exposed to surge.
The conspicuous orange spine at the base of the tail is venomous
and capable of causing painful wounds.

Acanthurus sohal (40 cm), in 1 m, Sharm-el-Sheikh, Red Sea, Egypt.

Snapping shrimps live in a variety of habitats including sandy burrows, under rocks,
or in association with various organisms. This species is found on feather stars.

Crinoid Snapping Shrimp, *Synalpheus* sp. (2 cm), in 15 m, Tulamben, Bali, Indonesia.

Harems consisting of numerous females and relatively few males
typify the social structure of *Paracheilinus* wrasses. The male
Eightline Flasher can intensify its fin coloration to arouse mating partners.

Paracheilinus octotaenia (8 cm), 15 m, Sharm-el-Sheikh, Red Sea, Egypt.

Crustaceans possess the ability to regenerate a missing appendage.
The reef lobster in this photograph lacks one of its giant chelipeds,
or pincers, possibly lost while defending itself.

Hairy Reef Lobster, *Enoplometopus occidentalis* (12 cm), in 20 m, Tulamben, Bali, Indonesia.

Squirrelfishes hide during the day and emerge at dusk to feed.
The night colours, shown here, are less intense than those apparent during the day.
Red is a dominant colour in squirrelfishes and several other nocturnal groups.

Longspine Squirrelfish, *Holocentrus rufus* (25 cm), in 12 m, Cayman Islands.

Sand flats are inhabited by the bizarre Spanner Crab, an edible and
much sought-after crustacean. The walking legs are flattened, forming blade-like
segments used for digging, enabling the animal to reverse quickly into the substrate.

Ranina ranina, (15 cm), in 11 m, Tulamben, Bali, Indonesia.

Opposite: This unusual fish not only resembles a snake, but also has
venomous fangs like its reptilian counterpart. Unlike other blennies,
this rarely seen species lives in muddy burrows and is nocturnally active.

Snake Blenny, *Xiphasia setifer* (35 cm), in 12 m, Anilao, Philippines.

Only the protruding, small black eyes reveal this crab's identity. Otherwise
it is easily mistaken for an algae-covered rock. The body's numerous spines and
tubercles, resembling algae, are responsible for its deceptive appearance.

Rock Crab, *Parthenope* sp. (4 cm), in 12 m, Kunkungan Bay, Sulawesi, Indonesia.

A male Mandarinfish flashes its mix of colours to attract females.
This spectacular display is seen at dusk. At other times it leads a
secretive lifestyle, moving over the bottom with a strange hopping motion.

Synchiropus splendidus (4 cm), in 2 m, Palau.

Delicate pastels dominate the pattern of Klunzinger's Wrasse,
a fish restricted to the Red Sea. Most other members of this
common Indo-Pacific group display a range of bold colours.

Thalassoma klunzingeri (15 cm), in 5 m, Sharm-el-Sheikh, Red Sea, Egypt.

Opposite: This sheltered, brackish lake has evolved a unique biological community.
Species diversity is very low, but the few organisms present are abundant.
Its mangrove fringe is shrouded in a tapestry of competing sessile organisms.

Kakaban Island, Kalimantan, Indonesia.

A coral reef is the marine equivalent of a desert oasis. Nutrient-poor tropical
seas contrast with expansive shallows where sunlight and recycled organic matter
promote rich algal growth, the first step in a complex food chain
involving an incredible abundance of life forms.

Aerial, Palau.

The bright colours and markings of many crustaceans, such as this
hippolytid shrimp, make easy targets for the many diurnal fish enemies.
Crabs, shrimps, and lobsters have evolved nocturnal habits as a means of survival.

Yellowspot Reef Shrimp, *Parahippolyte uveae* (5 cm), in 3 m, Sandfly Passage, Solomon Islands.

Mantis shrimps are voracious predators, feeding on other crustaceans and
small fishes. The swollen, hammer-like second legs are used to thump their prey
with a disabling blow. Known in parts of Southeast Asia as "Mike Tyson" shrimps.

Red Mantis Shrimp, unidentified squillid (4 cm), in 12 m, Madang, Papua New Guinea.

Opposite: Sheer dropoffs support vast numbers of small fishes,
such as the basslets seen here. Currents wash the reef walls with
a rich plankton soup, nourishing far greater numbers than usual.

Mixed fairy basslets, anthiids (each 6 cm), in 12 m, Madang, Papua New Guinea.

Night diving is a good way to find some of the reef's rarest and most beautiful
creatures, particularly crustaceans. The Orangenet Hingebeak Shrimp was discovered
and photographed for the first time on a nocturnal dive at Madang, Papua New Guinea.

Rhynchocinetes sp. (4 cm), in 15 m.

Unlike other anglerfishes, the Sargassumfish spends its life on the surface. It lives
and moves among floating rafts of weed, from which it takes its common name.

Histrio histrio (12 cm), surface, Maumere, Flores, Indonesia.

Every coral formation provides a home for a unique combination
of organisms. Representatives of widely different phyla coexist in peaceful
harmony, in spite of contrasting levels of evolutionary development.

Black coral, *Antipathes* sp.; tunicate, *Rhopalaea* sp.; Longnose Hawkfish, *Oxycirrhites typus* (7 cm);

unidentified sponge, in 45 m, Tulamben, Bali, Indonesia.

Coral reefs yield an unending procession of interesting discoveries,
large and small. Despite 30 years of diving experience, the author
found this colourful alga for the first time on a recent trip to Indonesia.

Unidentified green alga, possibly *Bornetella* sp. or *Neomeris* sp. (3 cm), in 3 m, Tulamben, Bali, Indonesia.

The photographer's flash brings to life the normally unseen spectrum of dazzling red.
This school of unusual snappers appears as dull brown fishes to the diver.

Schooling pinjalos, *Pinjalo lewisi* (30 cm), in 15 m, Walindi, Papua New Guinea.

Most tunicates found on coral reefs are small and directly attached
to their substrate. This one is unusual in both its large size and
in being supported by a stalk that each colony itself generates.

Bottlebrush Ascidian, *Neptheis fascicularis* (colony 40 cm), in 15 m, Komodo, Indonesia.

Hard corals derive their name from the rigid skeleton composed of calcium carbonate.
Each formation represents a colony of living animals or polyps, housed in separate
compartments. In many species they are seldom visible except at night when feeding.

Magenta-tipped Coral, *Acropora millepora* (entire colony 40 cm), in 8 m, Russell Islands, Solomon Islands.

This unique white Humpback Whale, a modern version of Moby Dick, was
first sighted off southern Australia five years ago. It is now regularly seen
thousands of kilometres further north during its annual migration to the tropics.

Megappera novaeangliae (12 m), Great Barrier Reef, off Cairns, Australia. Photo by Nobuo Suda.

When viewed head-on, it is unlikely any small fish or crustacean
would recognize the ominous danger posed by the Ambon Scorpionfish.
The long, curving handlebar 'eyebrows' contribute to its amazing camouflage.

Pteroidichthys amboinensis (10 cm), in 10 m, Lembeh Straits, Sulawesi, Indonesia.

Opposite: The camera's strobe momentarily illuminates tiny transparent sea squirts,
revealing a vivid neon network on an underwater Christmas tree. Also known as
ascidians or tunicates, these animals are common in all marine habitats.

Stalked ascidians, *Perophora namei* (field of view, 3 cm), in 8 m, Tolandono, Tukang Besi, Indonesia.

Wrasses are extremely numerous on coral reefs. Each species
exhibits well-defined preferences regarding bottom type and depth.
The Sixbar Wrasse occurs exclusively in shallow water.

Sixbar Wrasse, *Thalassoma hardwicke* (12 cm), in 2 m, Tulamben, Bali, Indonesia.

Opposite: The world's most ornate octopus still awaits scientific discovery,
although underwater photographs have alerted scientists of its existence. It has been
recorded so far from scattered localities in the western Pacific and Southeast Asia.

Ornate Octopus, *Octopus* sp. (15 cm), in 3 m, Lembeh Straits, Sulawesi, Indonesia.

This nudibranch seems oblivious to the shrimp passenger on its back
(and another hidden from view). Imperial Shrimps are commensal
with several types of sea slugs and holothurians.

Nudibranch, *Tambja* sp. (9 cm); Imperial Shrimp, *Periclimenes imperator* (1.5 cm), in 25 m,

Lembeh Straits, Sulawesi, Indonesia.

The fleshy inner mantle of a cowry secretes the calcium carbonate matrix
of the shell. Occasionally this structure can be seen enveloping the
outer surface and is responsible for maintaining the shell's brilliant lustre.

White-spotted Cowry, *Cypraea cribraria* (3 cm), in 8 m, Russell Islands, Solomon Islands.

The Titan Triggerfish employs a clever strategy to feed on sea urchins.
It picks up the urchin with its mouth, juggles it until the toxic spines
are facing downwards, and pushes it into the sand. Then it leisurely
penetrates the exposed underbelly, feasting on the internal organs.

Balistoides viridescens (40 cm), in 3 m, Tulamben, Bali, Indonesia.

Opposite: Dead protruding branches of black corals and gorgonians
are common on steep slopes. They provide a perch for filter-feeding
organisms to reach a favourable position for access to plankton-rich currents.

Encrusted antipatharian: hydroid, unidentified; red sponge, *Ectyodoryx* sp.; tunicates, *Clavalina* sp. and
Ectinascidea sp.; (colony 15 cm), in 20 m, Maumere, Flores, Indonesia.

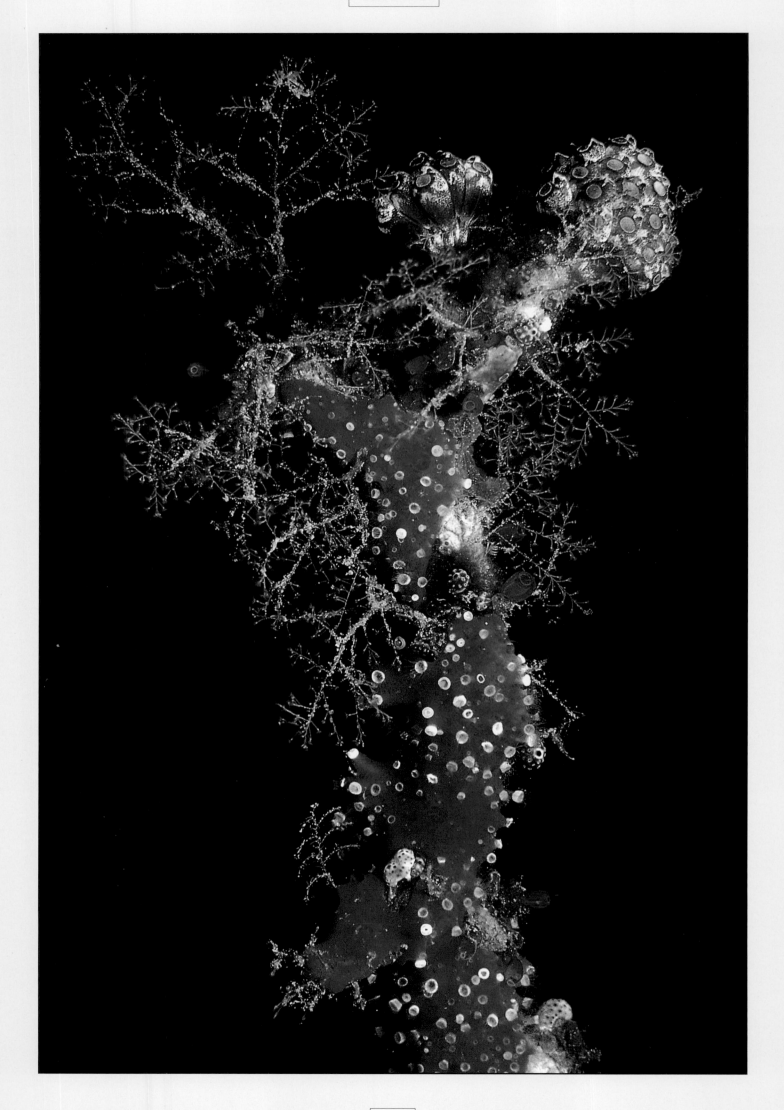

Bryozoans consist of colonies of numerous microscopic animals
known as zooids. Their ciliated tentacles, seen here
with the aid of a telephoto lens, are used to capture food.

Lace Bryozoan, *Triphyllozoon* sp. (10 cm), in 18 m, Ambon, Indonesia.

The Zebra Crab lives with sea urchins, clinging onto the spines with special hooklets
on the tips of its legs. This egg-carrying female is associated with the toxic
Ornate Sea Urchin. The dark colour of the eggs indicates they will soon hatch.

Zebra Crab, *Zebrida adamsii* (1.5 cm); Ornate Sea Urchin, *Asthenosoma varium*, in 16 m, Ambon, Indonesia.

Sea squirts are difficult to identify underwater, even by trained specialists.
Although they appear to have distinctive shapes and colours,
there is often considerable variation within a single species.

Pastel Sea Squirt, *Rhopalaea crassa* (2 cm), in 15 m, Komodo Islands, Indonesia.

The Red Sea and Arabian Gulf are home to many unique fishes.
The Blue Sailfin Tang is the most colourful member of the genus *Zebrasoma*.

Zebrasoma xanthurum (10 cm), in 12 m, Sharm-el-Sheikh, Red Sea, Egypt.

Deep crevices, such as the one seen here on the Great Barrier Reef, form an integral
part of the coral reef environment, providing shade and shelter for a diversity of life.
Ribbon Reef, Australia.

Opposite: The Adhesive Anemone assumes a convoluted shape
when it begins to retract. It can rapidly withdraw into the cranny
where it is anchored. In spite of its short, extremely sticky tentacles,
it can be inhabited by at least one species of anemonefish.
Cryptodendrum adhaesivum (40 cm), in 10 m, Tulamben, Bali, Indonesia.

Parasite-removing cleaner shrimps enter the mouths of ferocious predators
with impunity. Sometimes, in the company of cleaner fishes,
they maintain permanent stations where their vital service is performed.

Dark-spotted Moray, *Gymnothorax fimbriatus* (60 cm); Cleaner Shrimp, *Lysmata amboinensis* (5 cm), in 25 m,

Tulamben, Bali, Indonesia.

Appearances can be deceiving. The slow-swimming Yellow Boxfish
seems highly vulnerable, but is equipped with a bony carapace. It can also
secrete a potent skin toxin known as ostracitoxin, a genuine deterrent to predators.

Ostracion cubicus (3 cm), in 5 m, Green Island, Great Barrier Reef, Australia.

Flashlight Fishes live deep in reef crevices, emerging at night. At this time,
legions of these 10-centimetre long creatures literally light up the reef. Their most
distinctive feature is a large light organ under the eye, which contains luminous bacteria.

Photoblepharon palpebratus (10 cm), in 18 m, Tulamben, Bali, Indonesia.

Opposite: A close-up view of the central disc of a feather star reveals
a pair of white worms. In spite of their unusual shape, they have legs,
enabling them to move quickly over the host.

Feather Star Worm, myzostomid (7 mm), in 15 m, Tulamben, Bali, Indonesia.

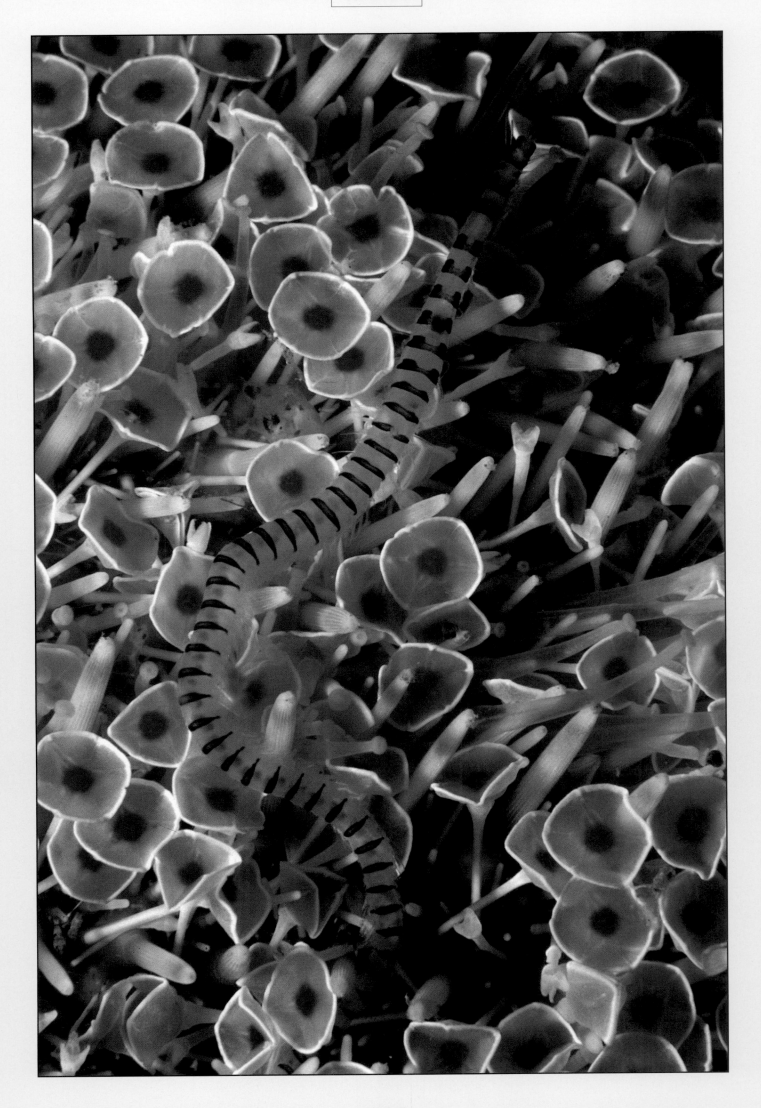

This pygmy angelfish is one of the sea's most difficult photographic targets.
It lives in the shadows of caves and crevices on walls and slopes
throughout the western and central Pacific.

Multi-barred Angelfish, *Centropyge multifasciatus* (7 cm), in 18 m, Walindi, Papua New Guinea.

Opposite: The pedicellariae of the Toxic Urchin deliver an excruciating sting
to careless divers. It was therefore surprising to witness this
small polychaete worm, which was unharmed when it contacted the urchin.

Toxic Urchin, *Toxopneustes pileolus* (10 cm); polychaete worm, *Typosyllis* sp. (5 cm), in 3 m,
Lembeh Straits, Sulawesi, Indonesia.

Shame-faced crabs fold their large flattened claws into the body,
as though hiding their face in shame. They are also called box crabs.
These animals inhabit a variety of bottom types, including sand, rocks, and coral.

Calappa sp. (8 cm), in 2 m, Ambon, Indonesia.

Abalone are readily recognised by the series of holes in the shell.
These function as outlets for water that is used for respiration.
With increased shell growth, new holes are formed and old ones are sealed.

Haliotis sp. (4 cm), in 12 m, Tulamben, Indonesia.

A close-up view of the disc-edge of this strange anemone reveals its unusual structure.
Its potent stinging cells are housed within grape-like nematospheres.

Hemprichi's Anemone, *Heterodactyla hemprichii* (disc 30 cm), in 8 m, Lembeh Straits, Sulawesi, Indonesia.

Colour pattern differences between sexes are apparent
in most types of wrasses, such as this female Vermiculate Wrasse.
Later it may change sex and assume more brilliant colours.

Macropharyngodon bipartitus (7 cm), in 12 m, Sharm-el-Sheikh, Red Sea, Egypt.

PHOTOGRAPHIC DETAILS

The photos in this book were taken with a 35 mm reflex camera in an underwater housing and 100 ASA film. Lenses utilized were 14 mm, 20 mm, 24 mm, 28-70 mm, 60 mm macro and 105 mm macro. A 2X converter was used in conjunction with the 105 mm lens for the super-macro shots. The 14 mm lens was used for wide-angle natural-light scenes and the surface reflection images. The half-in half-out photos were made with a 20 mm lens using one half of a +4 diopter lens in conjunction with one half of a polarizing filter to balance focus and exposure between the above- and below-water portions of the image. The microscopic pictures were shot on an optical bench system with tungsten 100 ASA film.

I use a single flash almost exclusively. It is mounted directly on top of the camera housing without cumbersome flash arms. Occasionally, for wide-angle shots, I use twin flashes.

I extend an invitation for readers to write with information on new marine discoveries or interesting observations on the behaviour of marine creatures.

Roger Steene
Box 188
Cairns QLD 4870
Australia